JESSIE KYD is one of the foun‹
organisation set up to support ¡
false allegations of abuse. Afte
Jessie has now returned to th
rural England with her family and various animals. She
is hoping to continue her newfound love of writing, while
continuing to help others who have been affected by false
abuse allegations.

www.facebook.com/KydJessie
www.twitter.com/KydJessie

THE Perfect SCAPEGOAT

JESSIE KYD

SilverWood

Published in 2016 by SilverWood Books

SilverWood Books Ltd
14 Small Street, Bristol, BS1 1DE, United Kingdom
www.silverwoodbooks.co.uk

Copyright © Jessie Kyd 2016

The right of Jessie Kyd to be identified as the author of this work has been asserted in accordance with the Copyright, Designs and Patents Act 1988 Sections 77 and 78.

All rights reserved. No part of this publication may be reproduced, stored in a retrieval system, or transmitted in any form or by any means, electronic, mechanical, photocopying, recording or otherwise, without prior permission of the copyright holder.

All essential facts are presented exactly as happened, but all names have been changed for the purpose of protecting the privacy of the child.

ISBN 978-1-78132-544-5 (paperback)
ISBN 978-1-78132-545-2 (ebook)

British Library Cataloguing in Publication Data
A CIP catalogue record for this book is available from the British Library

Page design and typesetting by SilverWood Books
Printed on responsibly sourced paper

*For Oliver – you have restored my self-belief
For my parents – you have supported me tirelessly
I would not have survived this journey without you all*

One

It was summertime. I don't really remember what the weather was like, whether it was a scorcher of a summer or a typical English washout, although I suspect the latter. For me there were more important things to think about – I was sixteen years old and waiting, with trepidation, for my exam results.

I had worked hard for my exams, revising every free moment I had, for hours on end some evenings, and well into the night. I was determined to do well, and had been predicted a good set of results by my teachers. Don't get me wrong; I was by no means a teacher's pet – in many ways I was quite the opposite in fact, somewhat of a rebel – but I did appreciate the need to achieve and had really knuckled down and applied myself throughout my school years. I was a confident person, perhaps something of an extrovert, and definitely nonconformist! I liked to do things differently, just because I could, but admittedly this didn't always receive the approval of my teachers! They knew I was bright, though, and I think they tried to see past my somewhat rebellious streak.

From about the age of thirteen or so I had experimented with different fashions, and eventually settled on the 'black look', or gothic as it was otherwise known. On one occasion I had decided that it would be a good idea to dye my beautiful sleek auburn hair, and much against the wishes and advice of my parents (who it has to be said were rather conservative and therefore quite shocked by my nonconformist ways!) I bought some black hair dye and assumed that I would end up with a fantastic new hair colour. But this idea ended in tears, my hair became rather straw-like and navy blue in colour and it looked awful for several weeks until the dye had completely washed out! Looking back I'm quite sure I didn't particularly like my appearance at the time, but it did stand out, and I think I probably enjoyed the attention I got, albeit rather negative. Looking back at photographs taken at the time, I can thankfully report that the 'black look' was very short lived, and I swiftly applied a more natural and conservative approach to my dress sense once more.

I recall the day of my exam results well, as if it was yesterday (isn't it funny how some things stay in your memory for ever, yet other, sometimes more recent things disappear completely?). I was petrified about going up to school, having spent the previous agonising weeks convincing myself that I must have failed at least some if not all of my exams. But I eventually plucked up the courage and cycled the short distance to school on my racing bike. I'd been given it for my sixteenth birthday and it was my most prized possession at that time – I thoroughly enjoyed using it as a means to keep fit and also for getting around quicker. Having hated games lessons at school, never being picked for teams with huge competitiveness among some pupils, I found myself extremely motivated by the arrival of my bike, and would regularly cycle ten or more miles each day. It turned out that I really was quite sporty, but had needed something to participate in without the added pressure of being picked for a team.

The first person I encountered was our headmaster. He and I had never really got on terribly well. I think he disliked my slightly rebellious attitude, in spite of the fact that I was very clever. Instead he preferred the pupils who were more traditional in their approach. But in fairness to him, he greeted me with a smile and told me that I needn't look quite so worried. He must have known our results before we did.

And he was right. I had achieved As and Bs in all but one subject (music was a D, but I will not dwell on this for too long!), and I recall that I had come third in our whole year, which I was very happy with. I had expected the two who had beaten me to do just that; they were both very hard workers. I will admit to feeling disappointed with my music result though, mainly because I had been expected to do well and I felt as if I had let my teacher down, but also because I had actually worked hard to prepare for the exam. I played both piano and oboe, but in truth I absolutely hated the oboe. It was a tough instrument to master, and I had struggled with it from day one; correct breathing style was vital and I just could not grasp it. Perhaps my poor result reflected this, but I was very chuffed to have done so well in the other subjects and I knew my parents would be too.

So now I had the rest of the summer ahead of me with no schoolwork to think about, no homework to do, and no essential music practice to do either.

I heard that there was a Saturday job available in one of

our village shops. The thought of earning some money of my own was very appealing, and that, combined with the thought of easing the boredom which was already beginning to set in, was enough to persuade me to call in to the shop and enquire about it. I'd never been in to the shop until now; it sold wool and a few other bits and pieces, and I'd never had the need. I met the owner, a woman called Sally, and sure enough she told me that she needed a Saturday person to work in the shop. It was agreed that I would start the following week.

I am not somebody who copes particularly well with change or new situations, so the week leading up to my new job starting was a fairly anxious one. My first Saturday afternoon arrived after a rather long week and, after a nervous period of learning the ropes, I found that I actually rather enjoyed serving customers and dealing with the sometimes mundane life of a shopkeeper. There really wasn't much to it, the anticipation and build up in my head had been far worse than the reality of what I was taking on. I needed to learn to work the till; by today's standards it was not particularly high tech but it was fairly modern for the time. I quickly got the hang of it, after a few initial mistakes (I couldn't always get the till to open when I wanted it to!), and couldn't believe how anxious I had been feeling.

There were many regular customers, and over the summer months I got to know lots of people from the village and surrounding areas. Some even became quite good friends, which was an added bonus. Admittedly a lot of the customers were much older than me, having perhaps retired to the village, but meeting people from all different walks of life made my time at work very enjoyable; I was very much a 'people person', and would always try to find something nice to say about everyone I met.

That summer turned out to be a particularly happy time in my life; I was sixteen and gaining a little bit of independence, which felt very grown up. I was probably the most content I had ever been, carefree, with no responsibilities yet and with only exciting times ahead. Life really didn't get much better than this!

We had moved to the village when I was ten years old, but only from a few miles down the road, and so the move hadn't ended up being as traumatic as I thought it would be. I remember feeling sad to be leaving behind some lovely friends who lived nearby and who I went to primary school with, and the thought of trying to make new friends and fit in scared me very much. My parents had decided to move house partly to ensure that we would be in the catchment area of their choice of secondary school for me, which I would go to a year or so after we arrived in the village. My older brother was already attending the school, and he had had a few traumatic experiences travelling on the bus to school each day, and I think this had also influenced my parents' decision to move nearer to the school. Some of the older children would pick on the younger ones, sometimes taking their lunch money from them and generally just being mean. My brother had found this pretty upsetting and my parents probably worried that I would too if I ended up having to take the bus to school.

When I eventually started at the secondary school I was over the moon to realise that some old friends from my previous school were attending as well. I felt very excited – and very important too, as I now had two lots of friends, and was the only one able to introduce them all to each other.

It was a lovely village to grow up in. In those days, which seem like a long time ago now, life felt very much safer than it does today. We children were fortunate enough to have a reasonable amount of freedom without parents worrying too much about where we were. There was a playground in the village with the usual swings, slides and roundabouts, but there was also an amazing park, full of hills, trees and exciting places to hide. In the winter, if we were lucky enough to get some snow, all of the local children would congregate there to go sledging. We really did have some fun, and we would always head back to somebody's house for a warm drink afterwards. In the summertime we would go to the park for walks or picnics. We all felt very safe, perhaps naively, but nothing horrid ever happened to any of us.

I also made some great friends in the village, all girls around the same age as me. Some of them were already very interested in boys at what seemed to me to be a very young age, with some of them having quite serious relationships before we even left school, but I just wasn't interested until some years later. I'm sure I didn't have a serious relationship until I was at least eighteen years old, although we did have a French exchange student at school for a few weeks and he was rather dashing, to say the least! But I must have been only thirteen or so at that time, and was happy to watch him from a safe distance, while some of my friends were a little more adventurous! They would flirt madly with him, and one girl even asked him out on a date, which I thought was totally unacceptable. I was so very naïve and I suppose rather traditional; it ought to be the boy asking the girl out on a date, not the other way round!

To start with I saw very little of the people who owned the shop. Sally, as a mother of three young children, was more often than not at home, which was on the outskirts of the village and quite a walk away. The shop was right in the centre of the village, nestled among several other small businesses. Her youngest child, Milly, was just a tiny baby when I started working for her parents, and probably took up most of her time. The middle child, a boy, was called Thomas, and he must have been two or three years old. The oldest child, Sarah, was a girl of around six or maybe seven years. I rarely saw Sally's husband, Jim. He worked fairly locally, doing some kind of manual work, but he was also a keen football player, which I soon realised took precedence over almost everything else, including pretty much every evening and weekend. I really couldn't see the appeal in the game, and I did feel sorry for Sally, as she seemed to see very little of her husband and had no help looking after the children – until I came along. I initially found Sally to be quite a scary character; she was one of those people who called a spade a spade, and she was quite a stern and serious person. On more than one occasion, when she and I had been in the shop together, she had spoken in a rather abrupt manner to a customer, and it had taken me aback. But I soon realised that customers knew to expect this from her; in fact over time a few customers confided in me that they would only come to the shop if they knew somebody else would be working! I thought Sally's attitude was unnecessary and it quite embarrassed me, but it really would have been more than my jobsworth to say anything. She was always polite to me, but definitely not the sort of person to tell me that I was doing well, or that she was pleased with me. A hard taskmaster perhaps, but over time that would change.

Soon enough not only was I working my hours in the shop, but I started being asked to help out at Sally and Jim's house with Thomas and Milly, too. I had been invited to the house after work a few times for a cup of tea, and had met both of the younger children. At this point I rarely saw Sarah though. I think she spent a lot of time with other family members, certainly her grandparents, or perhaps some of her own friends. I really didn't mind working more hours, though – the summer was dragging on and I had nothing else to do. My local friends were all busy earning money at their own part-time jobs, so I couldn't see much of them anyway. My parents were both working, and although mum only worked part-time the house was empty some of the time. I know some people enjoy their own company and thrive on being on their own, but I wasn't like that. I needed to be around people.

I quickly became quite fond, not only of the children, but of the whole family. Sally, although quite serious, was kind to me; over time she had softened and appeared to appreciate my help. Unfortunately, though, my time looking after the children was not always rewarded, and pay was infrequent. I had known from the outset what my hourly rate would be for hours worked in the shop, but we had never discussed what I would be paid for looking after the children. I suppose I assumed I would be paid at the same rate. I couldn't bring myself to ask for the money I believed I had earned, as Sally seemed so grateful to me and so busy, so I regularly came away at the end of the week with a lot less than I had been expecting to be paid. My parents felt that my generosity towards the family was hugely taken advantage of. And perhaps they were right; in truth I was paid virtually nothing for helping with the children. On the occasions that I was paid, £5 was the maximum amount I ever received, and that was for an entire day, working from around 9am until 6 or 7pm some evenings. I'm not sure how much that would equate to these days, but it probably was the equivalent of 'slave labour'! I'm sure Sally didn't ever intend to take advantage of me, but over time it did begin to feel like that. I was only sixteen years old, and this was my first ever job. While I had mountains of confidence in other situations, I could not bring myself to question the amount I was being paid, certain that the end result would be losing my job.

I saw little of Jim. As I have already said, he was usually out, either working or playing football. He seemed a quiet man, with few friends, and he certainly had eyes only for his two younger children. Thomas and Milly were spoilt in every way imaginable; they were forever eating sweets that he had given them, or being given other sorts of treats. By contrast he spent virtually no time with their big sister Sarah, other than occasionally asking her if she had had a good day at school, but even that was said from afar. It was strange to say the least, but I had been told by Sally from the outset that her husband struggled to cope with their daughter.

Sarah had special needs, both physically and mentally, which were quite profound. Her communication skills were fairly limited, although at school she was learning a basic form of sign language called Makaton, and this was helping to open up the world for her. I think her understanding was still basic, but having said that she was still more than capable of making her feelings known! She had learned to walk independently, but was fairly awkward and would take a tumble from time to time.

I don't recall ever seeing Jim give Sarah a kiss or a cuddle. Whether she understood his distant attitude towards her,

I don't know, but even so I always worried that she must have noticed she was treated differently to her siblings. I never saw Sarah approach her dad or show any interest in him either; perhaps she did understand and this was her way of dealing with it, I don't know. It was as if there was an unspoken understanding between them – you stay away from me and I'll stay away from you. Such a great pity, but looking back now I'm sure that having a child with such special needs would take its toll, and keeping his distance was just Jim's way of coping.

And so the summer passed. Towards the end of the holidays I think I must have made the grade working in the shop, as I was regularly asked to work extra hours. Having also got to know Sally and the children quite well by this time (and having met several members of the extended family), I had begun to spend more and more time with Thomas and Milly and also with Sarah, when she was at home. I think Sally appreciated the extra pair of hands, especially when all three children were at home. Things must have been difficult, although I never once heard her complain. I had always liked children, and was not bothered one bit by Sarah's disabilities, although some people would be visibly scared of her when we were out and about together. I think I was able to see the little person inside who was struggling to make sense of the world, whereas others struggled to see past the disabilities. Sarah had such a lovely character; she was a caring and compassionate little girl, with a great sense of humour, and these were the qualities I saw the more time I spent with her during that summer. I really think her disabilities frustrated her at times; she wanted to be able to communicate more effectively but had to rely purely on sign language; she wanted to be able to run and jump like those around her, but her legs just weren't strong enough. These frustrations would present themselves in quite severe tantrums, and these might last for some time. I tried to always be there for her, though, and would give her a big hug to let her know I cared.

As the holidays ended and September approached, I prepared to take up my studies once more. I would be studying at the local college for the next two years. No more school uniform from now on and I would take the bus in to our local town each day, which I was quite excited about.

Having a little more freedom now than I had had at school, my attitude towards college work, I must admit, was not great, pretty much from the outset. I was perfectly content doing just enough work to get by rather than striving to achieve the very best I was capable of. We had some free periods most days, but I preferred to walk into the local town to do some window-shopping rather than make better use of my time and study. I bitterly regret now the change in my attitude, but of course teenagers don't like being told what to do and certainly don't ever admit to being wrong! I'm sure my parents must have felt very frustrated but there was nothing they could do other than offer advice, which I obviously took no notice of.

I think one factor contributing largely to the change in my attitude was my choice of subjects. I struggled quite a bit from day one with one of the subjects in particular, history. Rather than admit my mistake though, I plodded on, hating every lesson and not taking anything in at all. The teacher was very boring too, and taught in a rather old-fashioned manner, which undoubtedly made things even worse. I just couldn't get excited about the past. The teacher talked, without ever using any visual aids or props, and we were expected to make copious notes with which to go home and write essays. I don't think I ever wrote a good one. I really should have taken the bull by the horns and asked if I could study something different, but I didn't.

My commitment to studying, or lack of, was also not helped by the fact that I was spending more and more time working in the shop and helping out with the children. Sally seemed to need more and more help dealing with the demands of juggling family life and the business, and Jim seemed unable to deal with Sarah's disabilities, which only served to increase the pressure that Sally was under. Both parents seemed to have become somewhat dependent on me, which I have to admit I quite liked. They certainly encouraged me to spend more or less all of my free time with them, even though they knew that I had college work to do. Perhaps I wasn't honest about the amount of homework that was expected of us; I should have been.

My own parents, however, were becoming more and more concerned about the amount of time I was spending with Sally and her family, not least because it was affecting my college work and my grades. They also felt very strongly that I was being taken advantage of, and in truth of course they were right. I think I realised that myself, but I allowed it to happen nonetheless as Sally seemed to need me more than ever. I remember more than one occasion when my dad called in to the shop and asked Sally and Jim for their support in encouraging me to spend less time with them and more time at college, or at home studying. But of course this did not happen. They knew that I enjoyed my time with them as much as they enjoyed having me around to help. It suited them so why would they encourage anything to change?

I think to a degree, being the rebellious teenager I was, that the more my parents pushed for me to reduce the amount of time I spent with the family, the more time I decided I was going to spend with them. I wanted to wind my parents up – because that's what teenagers do! Because of Sally and Jim's reluctance to cooperate with my parents, there was inevitably a great deal of tension between the two sets of adults, and more often than not, because they were my friends as opposed to my parents, I would take the side of Sally and Jim. As a result there was much friction when I was at home, and many heated conversations about the time I was spending with Sally and the children. I know now that these conversations were aimed at encouraging me to knuckle down and study and that my parents had the very best of intentions, but they failed miserably. I was getting by with average grades but at the same time was having fun with Sally, who by now had become a firm friend, even though she was a good few years older than me. My parents must have been so worried at the time, but I just refused to listen to them.

I gradually started to lose touch with my friends from school. I saw some of them from time to time around college, but none of them took the same subjects as me, and we all gradually grew apart. One of my school friends had had a baby within just a few months of us all leaving, and didn't ever start college, even though she was very bright. Another had gone to a different college. And so I guess it was inevitable that we would go our separate ways and form new friendship groups with people with whom we perhaps now had more in common.

Quite early on at college I became friends with a girl called Laura, who I met in one of my language classes. Laura was not as rebellious as me, but we still hit it off from day one and were regularly reprimanded for talking at the back of the French class. Our French teacher took a real dislike to me, and quite frankly I don't blame her! After all, I was always the instigator of our chats. I admit to being somewhat envious of Laura, as she had her own motorbike, and although I had learned to drive as soon as I turned seventeen, I didn't actually pass my test until I was nineteen and so had to catch the bus to college each day. I was a little jealous too, as she was exceptionally bright and always did well. But I'm sure she must have worked hard, which was the difference between us. I expected to do well, but hardly did any work to achieve that.

Two years passed, and results day loomed once again. Laura's exam results were, as expected, straight As. My exam results, on the other hand, weren't so good. I hadn't achieved what the teachers had predicted in any of my subjects, although I had managed to pass everything, even history. I was indignant about my poor grades – I think I must have been in complete denial about the fact that I didn't actually deserve to do any better than this. And so I asked for the papers to be re-marked, assuming that a huge mistake had been made by whoever had marked each of them! The exam papers were duly sent away to be marked again – waiting for them was an agonising few weeks – but unfortunately the original results had been correct and my grades remained the same. Although my parents didn't ever say so, I'm sure they must have felt disappointed with my results, rightly so too. They knew that I was capable of so much more.

I had applied to various universities to study languages, but my grades were just not good enough, so I needed to make a tough decision. Should I retake my exams? Should

I try to get into a different university? Or should I do something else?

My heart just wasn't in it. I had no enthusiasm about going to university at all. I think this was partly because, from being a young child right through to being a teenager, I had never been that good about staying away from home, even just overnight. But the time I spent with Sally and the children, and how much I enjoyed it, now played a huge part in my lack of enthusiasm to go away too.

So I decided to take a year out and reapply to start a course the next year. I knew I would need to sell the idea to my parents, so I told them that I planned to study part-time and try to get an additional qualification, and I would also apply to do some voluntary work, which would undoubtedly look good on my CV. By this point in time I was already beginning to question whether languages were the best option anyway. I so enjoyed looking after Sarah, Thomas and Milly, and liked the idea of training to become a teacher of children with special needs. I had been in to the special school that Sarah attended several times, and had always felt really inspired to work with these children. I had learned a lot of the sign language which many of them were taught, which meant that I was able to communicate with them, an amazing feeling, especially seeing a face light up because I had understood what a child was signing. I felt completely in awe of the staff at the school too, who were so dedicated to and skilful at their work.

So, I took my year out. Although I did start some part-time studies, none of them lasted more than a couple of months at most. I went to college in the evenings to study psychology, which was actually very interesting. But once again my attitude was awful and I just didn't have the desire or commitment. On the other hand, though, I did do some voluntary work, and enjoyed it very much. I taught French at a local prep school. I went swimming with a group of children from Sarah's special school and I worked a few hours each week at a respite home for children with special needs. All of these I thoroughly enjoyed. The teaching experience was amazing, as I was allowed to prepare my own lesson plans each week and teach as if these were my own classes. I felt completely at ease, and really looked forward to these sessions. I enjoyed the other work too, and just knew from everything I was doing that working with children was what I wanted to end up doing eventually.

A large part of my week was still being spent with Sally and her family. I really did feel by now that they depended on me quite heavily, and I knew that Sarah's disabilities meant it was much harder for Sally to rely on just anyone to help out. At the same time I had formed quite an attachment to them all and did enjoy the feeling that I was helping out a family in need.

Neither Milly nor Thomas were yet at school and so were often at home during the day, apart from some mornings spent at preschool groups or mums 'n' tots. But I was quite happy just spending time with whoever was around; there were always people coming in and out of the house, and so there was always somebody to talk to.

My parents were right, though; I can see now that I was being taken advantage of so much by this time. I should have been let go by Sally and Jim – they should really have respected my parents' wishes – but the reality was that my presence was very convenient for them. If a carrot was offered in the form of even the smallest amount of money or, more frequently, a small gift, I would make myself available to them. At the expense of everything and everyone else. It wasn't even the case that I needed money for anything in particular. The more time went by, the more I somehow felt relied upon and needed, and this slowly but surely took precedence over all other aspects of my life.

Looking back, I can remember being given quite a few gifts by Sally over the years. These were never expensive gifts and sometimes they did not appeal to me at all, but nonetheless I saw them as a sign that the family thought highly of me, and this meant a great deal at the time. My mum clearly recalls the time when I arrived home with some rather cheap underwear that Sally had given me. I had no idea at the time, but mum was terribly upset that Sally had bought me something so personal – Sally was after all my boss and I think mum found it unprofessional. On other occasions I was given earrings and other jewellery, clothes, and little ornaments, more often than not gifts from the children. All of these things would make me feel needed and I guess valued, and of course there was no way I would even consider walking away from the family at this stage.

By now I think my mum was feeling threatened, too, as if her role as my mother was slowly being taken over. It didn't even cross my mind at the time, but looking back I can see now that she was right; Sally was monopolising me. I'm sure there was no malice in Sally's behaviour and that she did not intend to upset my mum, but all the same this situation did cause much sadness.

When I was nineteen, Sally and Jim asked me how I would feel about them going away on holiday for a few weeks and leaving the children in my care.

They planned to go abroad, I think to Portugal. Jim's love of football was at the centre of the holiday plans

(I think there were some 'important' matches that he wanted to go and see live), but I'm sure Sally saw it as an opportunity to spend some quality time with her husband. Why they couldn't take the children away for a family holiday I'm not sure, but the children were certainly not part of these holiday plans. Perhaps this was an adults-only holiday or perhaps they thought the children were too young yet to be taken away.

Needless to say, I jumped at the chance. The thought of being responsible for both the children and the shop for two or three weeks was a real thrill; I felt privileged to have been asked and I knew I was more than capable. I knew that leaving Sarah with anybody would be hard for Sally, though. She was in reality her sole carer, and dealt with every aspect of her care and needs; I cannot remember a time when Jim helped around the house or with Sarah. In his defence, he did spend time with the other two children, and would frequently take them off somewhere or other, to visit their grandparents, or just for a ride around, and I'm sure this must have eased the pressure for Sally somewhat. But he never went along to any of Sarah's medical appointments, which were fairly frequent, and I am certain that Sally must have felt very alone at times. Of course Sally's loyalty to her husband meant that she never complained.

By this time I had been helping the family out, both at home and in the shop, for around three years, and Sally must have felt confident in my abilities. I knew the workings of the business inside out; over time both Sally and Jim had shown me the ropes, including keeping the books up to date and balancing the till. I had also spent a huge amount of time with the children, so I was very familiar with their routines too.

The holiday came and went. Everything at the shop and the house ran smoothly and the children coped remarkably well without their parents. In order to cause a minimal amount of disruption to their lives, I stayed with them at their house. It was still term-time, and so Sarah was collected each morning by the school minibus and driven home each afternoon. Even with her disabilities, Sarah was a remarkably easy child to take care of. She enjoyed many of the things that other children her own age would enjoy, although some things would never be possible because of her limitations. One of her favourite pastimes was going to the playground and riding on the swings, and we would walk there regularly over the years. Sarah did tumble quite frequently, and I always felt terrible if this happened whilst she was in my care, as if it was somehow my fault, which of course it wasn't. She also had a tricycle, made especially for a child with special needs. Sarah adored riding this, although I remember many times when I had to run to keep up with her, petrified that she might somehow manage to tip herself out, which I'm sure would have been impossible.

In many ways we became inseparable. I know Sarah was very fond of me, perhaps because I treated her as far as possible exactly the same way I would treat any other child. I was very fond of her too. She taught me so much about so many things, not least that every person, no matter who they are and what they look like on the outside, is unique and has something to offer. We must look deeper inside that person, and there we will always find something very special.

Sarah and I also shared a love of food, and in particular sweet things! Given half a chance she would probably have chosen to live off ice cream and chocolate, but it was important for me not to indulge her too much. I knew that her life expectancy was not great, and for that reason it was very tempting to spoil her with things she enjoyed eating; but if Sarah gained too much weight her legs would not be able to carry her. They were not particularly strong anyway, but it would have been awful if she had been confined to a wheelchair. She would have hated it.

Thomas, too, was a very straightforward little boy. He loved being physically active, and was never happier than when he was playing out in the garden, as is typical of most boys.

Milly, on the other hand, was not quite as easy as her siblings. She and I had a good relationship, but I was not prepared to stand any nonsense from her, and for that reason she would often choose to spend time with her dad rather than me; he was a much softer touch than I was and would give in to her demands very easily. Jim was always happy to find some time for Thomas and Milly if they wanted to do things with him.

I can remember one of Sarah's birthdays when she actually spent the day with mum and me and her siblings at our house, rather than with her own parents. The children were very used to spending time at my parents' house; they had visited many times, usually when we had been out for a walk and we would call in to see my mum and have a drink on our way back to their house. But Sarah's birthday has stuck in my mind all these years – I always thought that each of her birthdays would have been celebrated to the fullest, particularly considering her special needs and knowing that she may sadly not reach adulthood. In my family, my parents always made a huge fuss about birthdays; presents, balloons and a cake were always a guaranteed part of the day. I suppose I assumed that all families were the same as mine. I have since met many who, like Sarah's family, do not treat the day quite as enthusiastically as mine did! Perhaps Sally had felt that Sarah would have more fun with us, and I'm sure we did make it a special day for her.

In the end I followed my heart and towards the end of my year out I applied to study for a teaching degree. The required grades turned out to be lower than for the language courses I had previously applied for, and so I was readily accepted on to my preferred course at my preferred university.

Laura had started at university the previous year, but she and I remained close friends. We wrote to each other during term-time, and met up during the holidays. Her parents were fairly local to where we lived, which made it easier to keep in touch. We mostly met up in the evenings, and went out to a local pub for a drink and a catch up. Once or twice we ventured to a nightclub, knowing full well that we both hated these sorts of places! But it seemed to be the thing that all the other teenagers were doing and so we thought we would find out for ourselves what the attraction was. But after an hour or so of sitting in a dark corner, we always decided that enough was enough, and scuttled off to the nearest pub! Although we liked boys and talked a lot about who we were keen on at that time, we decided it would be preferable to meet somebody likeminded, and that this was far more likely to happen at university! Ours was an amazing friendship, even though we were quite different in lots of ways. For us the important factor was that we had similar thoughts about things and could almost finish one another's sentences – we knew instinctively what the other was thinking.

Laura had met Sarah a few times during the previous two or three years; sometimes she and I would arrange to meet up for a coffee in a cosy café we both liked, but more often than not I would then be asked to look after Sarah on the same day. Rather than tell Sally I was unavailable, I would take Sarah with me to meet Laura. I think it made Sarah feel quite grown-up. Laura and I would sit chatting, drinking our hot chocolate, and Sarah would have one too. I think these times just made Sarah feel a little bit special and Laura was very easy-going and liked children, which helped.

Much to my parents' dismay, I was notified by the university that there was no accommodation available on campus, and that due to my proximity to the university (I actually lived some sixty miles away, but this was classed as close!), I would not be able to live on campus, at least for the first year. Now for me this was not a particular problem, and actually made the whole idea of going to university more bearable, but I knew my parents were keen for me to experience university life. For them this meant moving away from home, living with other students and generally fending for oneself. It would also mean severing my ties with Sally and the rest of the family, and for my parents this would have been an added bonus.

Sally and the children had become very attached to me; I had now spent over three years working for Sally and helping to look after the children, and having to live at home while I studied would mean that I would be able to see them all more often than if I was living at university. So I think Sally was secretly quite pleased. As I had by this time passed my driving test (third time lucky), I decided to commute daily until such time as student accommodation became available.

September arrived, and backwards and forwards to university I drove. My timetable was quite full and I had lectures every day. But the drive wasn't actually all that bad; I listened to the radio or my own music tapes, of which I had many.

My parents were chuffed to bits that I had started a university course, but they did worry that I was missing out on university life. I didn't ever stay behind after my lectures to go out for a drink with the other students. I always left as soon as the last lecture had finished, in the hope of seeing Sally and the children for an hour or so before the children went to bed.

The friends I made at university – there was a group of six of us – were all daily commuters. The others lived fairly locally, and they all went home at the end of the day, just as I did. I guess I probably subconsciously chose this group of friends for that very reason; we all had something in common. Two of the girls were mature students and had husbands and children at home, and the other three all lived with their parents. But even though we would all go home after lectures, we still had lots of fun, and we all became good friends. There was much banter between us. I was inevitably the butt of every joke, being the typical naïve country girl, while they were all city girls and much more worldly wise than I was. It was great fun, though, and I always looked forward to our time together.

I had already decided that I wanted to gain as much experience as possible of working with children with special needs, with the ultimate aim of working in a special school. The course I had chosen was packed full of work experience, and almost from the outset we were sent in to schools to try out our skills. The course was great, I loved it, but history did seem to be repeating itself when, at the end of the first year, my exam results were only just good enough to get me through to the second year of the course. I had literally just scraped through. I remember being quite indignant (once again!) about the results, but they did of course reflect the fact that my commitments at home still took up too much of my time at the expense of my studies.

As well as helping out in the shop and with the children, I was also asked to babysit for other families from time to time. I'm not sure that Sally was in favour of this – she seemed to see me as her personal helper, and I could sense her disapproval whenever I told her I had been asked to babysit for some other family – but for me it was additional pocket money and more experience gained. Babysitting was pretty mundane, though, as I was usually wanted in the evenings so that the parents could go out, and if the children weren't already in bed when I arrived, it would soon be their bedtime. Some houses where I babysat were quite scary and I had lots of funny experiences at others, too – in fact I did refuse to babysit for a second time for one or two families! One house where I babysat was very old; while it was still light outside everything was fine but as soon as it got dark I would hear all sorts of strange noises. Convinced that there was somebody other than me and the children in the house, I would creep from room to room searching, but of course never finding anybody. There was another family who had a cat, as we did, but for some reason I found I was allergic to this particular cat's fur and I had quite a nasty reaction to it, and ended up having to telephone my parents so that one of them could take me to the hospital for treatment, while the other parent remained at the house with the children...and cat!

That summer was a good one, but little did I realise at the time that it would be my last summer with Sally and the children.

Now that I could drive, I was able to take the children out for day trips, and that summer we went somewhere most weeks. Sally rarely came along on our days out; I think she was glad of a break, and she must have been able to get so much done in the house while we were away. The children always enjoyed our days out, and once we were home would tell Sally everything they had been doing. I tried to include Sarah in everything we did, and her excitement was clear to see whenever we went anywhere new; she thrived on the experiences I introduced her to. Milly and Thomas always coped well when we were out and about with Sarah, even though taking her with us inevitably slowed us up, and I'm sure they must have felt frustrated at times. They were obviously very fond of her.

Looking back, that summer, which was otherwise very happy, was the only time too that I was ever concerned about Sarah's well-being. At the time I couldn't put my finger on it, but I sensed that something was not right in her world. During one outing in particular, Sarah was subdued all day, and she wet her pants, something she never usually did. At the time I just thought she might be feeling unwell. How I wish I had paid more attention to her and perhaps somehow tried to find out what was wrong; I'm sure I even told her off for having wet pants. But by the next day she had thankfully been back to her normal self once more and so any concerns I had disappeared quickly too and I didn't give this incident another thought.

Just before the start of term I took Sarah, Thomas and Milly away for a short caravan holiday. Another friend of mine, Martha, came too. The children's parents hadn't taken them on holiday, but I had great memories of holidaying as a young girl, and thought that the children would enjoy some time away, which they did. We went swimming, we went for walks, we went to the beach, and generally just had a fun few days. Martha was a couple of years younger than me, but she and I had known each other for quite some time, and she also knew the children a little.

Around that time I also started taking Sarah to a group in the village put on for the local children, and Martha was a helper there, helping Sarah to integrate on the occasions when I was unable to go. I think the group was set up mainly for youngsters to meet up and have some fun, rather than risk them hanging around on street corners and getting into trouble. We went away on an overnight camp with this group too, which was fun, although I hadn't managed to get a great deal of sleep, surrounded as I was by lots of excitable children!

Sally had allowed Sarah to come on the overnight camp and she had seemed to enjoy it, as she generally seemed to enjoy the group, although it was not always easy to tell. She was very happy to go along to the weekly gatherings, and I think she would have tried to make her feelings known had she not wanted to. But she was rather mothered by the other children, especially the girls, and I'm not sure that was what she really wanted. They tended to speak to her as if she was much younger than she was, and this did result in aggressive outbursts from time to time. I was used to these by now but they must have shocked the other children. I'm sure if she could have communicated it, that Sarah would have told them all she wanted was to be treated the same as any other little girl.

September arrived and I carried on into my second year of studies. I did not even bother to enquire about the availability of accommodation on campus. I was happy commuting, and intended to carry on doing so. The winter months were tough, I will admit. Although I was a confident driver, I didn't enjoy driving if the roads were icy, but I always made it to university if I could, and more often than not I did get there. I would use the time in my car to reflect upon my life and whatever was going on at that time. If I had had a row with my parents, if I was worrying about my college work – this commuting time was perfect for working through and usually resolving things.

It was during this first term of my second year of studies that my life changed forever.

Two

"We are arresting you on suspicion of indecent assault. You do not have to say anything, but it may harm your defence if you do not mention when questioned something you later rely on in court. Anything you do say may be given in evidence."

I felt the room start to spin; everything was happening in slow motion. I stood, motionless, completely rooted to the spot, not wanting to believe what I was hearing. I was in a state of total shock and disbelief.

I remember clearly that it was a Wednesday, and that this was a day I was usually late coming home. But for some reason – as far as I remember, my afternoon lectures had been cancelled – I had arrived home early that day.

In fact, I can be very precise; it was the exact time that the local school finished for the day – I remember I drove past Sally walking home with Thomas and Milly. Sally didn't wave as she usually did, which I thought strange, but instead she lowered her head and seemed to pretend not to have seen me. Considering the events of the previous weeks, which become clear as I go on, I suppose I should not have been surprised, but I did feel incredibly hurt. Thomas and Milly were far too busy chatting with some of their friends to notice me, but that was fine. That was normal.

After catching up with mum for a while, I decided to have a much-needed bath. At the start of our course we had had to choose a subject in which to specialise so that we could become skilled in one particular area of teaching. I had chosen to specialise in P.E. (thinking that it would be much easier than other subjects, but I was also keen to try different sports) and we had been doing various group sports activities that morning. I was having a relaxing soak in the bath, trying to unwind after the sports and the long drive home, when I heard the doorbell ring. I didn't expect it to be anybody calling for me, as most of my friends were now themselves studying at university and lived quite a way away. I could hear a conversation taking place on the doorstep; perhaps it was one of mum's friends or a neighbour.

But very soon I heard a rather heated discussion taking place, and I could make out two other voices that were unfamiliar to me.

Mum came upstairs and knocked on the bathroom door. As I sat up she told me there were two police officers downstairs and that they wanted to talk to me.

I got out of the bath and quickly got dressed and came downstairs, at which point I was arrested.

In October, just a few weeks prior to my arrest, Sarah had been unwell. I think to begin with she had just had a cold, but her immune system wasn't that strong and her colds always seemed far worse than everyone else's. Her nose would run and run and run, and she would be completely bunged up.

Over a period of a week or so Sarah became more and more poorly. She was quite distressed and obviously felt absolutely rotten. I recall that she started struggling to go to the loo at this time too, and I'm sure this must have added to her discomfort. Constipation was not an unusual part of Sarah's existence, and we always tried to get her to eat as much fibre as possible, but she was more often than not pretty clogged up. We usually knew if she was particularly constipated, as she would put her hands between her legs and squeeze her legs together as hard as she could. She would sometimes sit and strain in this way for ages and ages, and would go very red in the face too. She might do it while sitting watching television, or when sitting at the table eating. Sally inevitably ended up telling her to stop, because she felt it was inappropriate anywhere other than when sitting on the loo. This telling off would more often than not result in Sarah crying; I think she endured quite a lot of pain when the constipation was especially bad and probably didn't really understand why Sally was reprimanding her for trying to make it better. Being a usual part of Sarah's life, though, constipation alone would not have caused too much concern, but this time she was also finding it difficult to go for a wee, which led to Sally eventually taking her in to hospital.

I knew Sarah had been taken to hospital because I had done my usual thing of calling in to their house when I arrived home from university one evening. But this particular evening Jim told me that Sally had taken Sarah to hospital. This was the first time in the four years I had known the family that Sarah's health had been this bad, but I assumed that whatever hospital treatment was needed would do the trick and that Sarah would be back home soon.

Sally arrived home later that evening, and I spoke to

her on the telephone to see how Sarah was. Sarah had been admitted to the children's ward and was going to be under observation for a few days until her condition improved.

I was sure that Sarah would give the staff at the hospital quite a hard time. She could be difficult. I had just got used to her ways over time and was capable of dealing with her. But the hospital staff did not know her at all, which must have made their job pretty tough, especially as she would have been feeling very unwell. It was at times like this that she might become aggressive and rather loud.

Sally asked me if I would be able to stay at the hospital with Sarah; this would help her out of a difficult situation, as she was needed at home to look after the other children. As usual I was more than happy to help out, and in the end I stayed at the hospital for two or three days and nights, once again at the expense of my studies. I stayed in Sarah's room (she had a room of her own), and slept on a comfy chair. Sarah slept on and off for much of the time, but when she was awake she was quite a handful.

It was a very long few days. I popped home once for some fresh clothes and a shower, but that was all. I was totally exhausted, but it was a nice feeling knowing that I was not only helping Sally but at the same time helping the hospital staff. If I hadn't been there they would inevitably have ended up having to spend a lot more time with Sarah, as I'm sure she would undoubtedly have tried to take advantage of them!

Sarah was diagnosed with a urinary tract infection, or UTI. Knowing what was wrong seemed to me to be positive – at least, I thought, she would now receive the relevant treatment and hopefully be back home soon. But things took an awful turn for the worse after her diagnosis.

After spending a couple of days at the hospital, I went for a walk from Sarah's room towards the main ward. As I walked past a room that had been empty the whole time I had been staying there, I saw Sally sitting talking to some other adults. They were not hospital staff – they were not dressed in hospital attire. I had no idea who they were, but Sally was visibly upset.

Rather than carry on walking to the ward, I turned back to Sarah's room and sat and waited for Sally to come back. I thought maybe they had found out something terrible and that Sarah was much more sick than any of us had known. My mind was racing by the time Sally arrived back at the room, alone now.

She looked awful. Her face was red and her eyes puffy from crying. It seemed like ages, but it was probably only a matter of minutes, before she spoke. She explained that when the paediatrician examined Sarah and diagnosed the infection, he found what he believed were signs of sexual abuse. The adults who had been talking to Sally were in fact social workers, now assigned to 'this case', as they called it.

I sat in silence, trying to take in what I was being told. Sarah was fast asleep and oblivious to the tension and upset in the room. She had been abused? When? By whom? So many things were rushing through my head, not least the fact that I just could not believe what I was hearing. How could she possibly have been abused? She was only ever with Sally or me when she was at home, and we didn't let her out of our sight, not until she was tucked up in bed at night. And during the day she was at school surrounded by adults we both liked and trusted. She spent time with her grandparents too, but all of these people we knew well. This couldn't possibly be true, could it?

This was the point at which everything changed.

Sally had been told, I presumed by the social workers, that the police would also be notified and that an investigation would be carried out. The paediatrician, I understood, wanted to carry out a more thorough examination of Sarah, an internal examination, I think, and there was talk of a police surgeon being involved too. They were intending to anaesthetise Sarah in order to reduce her stress levels during the examination. As far as I was aware, the only sign that the paediatrician had noted so far was soreness around her bottom, and I knew that this was fairly usual for Sarah and was caused by her ongoing constipation. I hoped so much that this horrible situation would all be cleared up quickly, and these people would realise that they had been wrong.

During the next few days, apart from snippets of information that Sally gave me, I was in the dark about what was happening. The hospital staff obviously weren't going to tell me anything as I was not related to Sarah, and Sally was quite understandably very preoccupied with everything she was having to deal with. I found this very hard to cope with, as I had been such a huge part of the family's lives, yet at this time of need I felt completely alone. All of a sudden I felt very isolated, and it was quite scary. I was scared for Sarah too – what was going to happen to her, would she be OK?

A day or so after I had received the news that Sarah may possibly have been abused, mum had come to the hospital to see how Sarah was. She and I were sitting in Sarah's room chatting when two police officers, one a WPC and the other a detective sergeant, knocked on the door. They asked me if I could spare a few minutes to chat to them, which of course I agreed to.

I was led to an empty room, and asked to sit down.

I must have been there for at least forty-five minutes, and I was grilled quite thoroughly about the concerns that had been raised. I told them of my belief that the soreness could well be as a result of chronic constipation, but I'm not sure that this possibility was taken on board. There didn't seem to be any doubt in the minds of these officers. It seemed to be a case of who had abused Sarah, not of establishing whether or not she had been abused, even at this early stage. I couldn't really offer any answers though; I had been racking my brains ever since receiving the news, trying to think of anybody who would have had (a) the opportunity and (b) the desire to do anything to hurt an innocent young girl. I felt myself starting to look at everybody we knew and question whether they might be a potential abuser, even though in my heart I could not believe it of any of them. At the time I did not feel as if the finger of blame was being pointed at me, but looking back, perhaps the police officers felt they might be able to trip me up if they took me to one side, pretending to be friendly and interested. I am also not certain, now, of the legalities of being interviewed in such a way. But at the time it was presented to me as an informal chat; it was not recorded and I was not under caution.

Having said that it was an informal chat, however, I found the whole forty-five minutes extremely stressful and, when I eventually returned to Sarah and my mum, I was in floods of tears. Sarah was sitting on my mum's knee when I got back; mum was also fond of her, having got to know her quite well during the time I had spent working for the family. But as soon as she saw me crying, Sarah bounced off mum's knee and came over and gave me a huge cuddle. Sarah was a very tactile little girl and liked nothing more than giving and receiving cuddles. She was worried to see me so upset; this was probably the first time ever that I had cried in front of her. I reassured her that I would be fine, and she settled down again.

Later that same day I sat in the hospital canteen with Sally; we sat mostly in silence, deep in our own thoughts, drinking our cups of tea. I turned to Sally at one point and asked her why she hadn't asked me if I had abused Sarah. She responded, "I don't need to ask you. I know you haven't done it." I told her that all I wanted to do was wrap Sarah up in a blanket and take her away from the hospital and this horrid situation we were faced with. Little did I realise that, in the weeks to come, this comment would be blown out of all proportion and used against me.

I called in to the shop the day before Sarah was discharged from hospital. There was nobody in the shop but I could hear voices in the room at the back. I could hear Jim talking to a woman; I recognised the voice but was unsure where I had heard it before. Then it came to me: it was one of the police officers I had talked to at the hospital. I wasn't sure whether or not it was appropriate to knock on the door and ask how the other children were, so I stood and waited for a minute or two to see if the conversation between the two was ending. In many ways I wish I hadn't waited, as I heard Jim telling the police officer that I was, "Behaving in a very guilty manner." He carried on, saying that he wasn't sure why I was behaving strangely, but he felt the officer would want to know. I left and walked all the way home in tears. I kept telling myself that perhaps I had misheard what Jim said, but I knew in my heart that I had heard him correctly.

With hindsight, perhaps I shouldn't really have been surprised to hear Jim talking the way he had. He had visited the hospital once while Sarah was there, and while there he had told me he knew categorically that the alleged abuse had not been committed by any family member. I remember thinking, how could he possibly know this?

In total, Sarah stayed in hospital for five days. Sally was able to bring her home once the UTI had cleared up. It must have been such a relief for them all to have her back at home, and well on the road to recovery. Apart from what was now happening, it had been a worrying few days.

I saw Sarah briefly on the afternoon she came home, as I was working in the shop that day. Thankfully, she seemed much more her old self and was pleased to see me. She was lying down on the settee in the sitting room – I guess she was pretty exhausted from her hospital stay. I went over to her and knelt down, telling her how nice it was to see her and that I hoped she would feel like getting out and about again soon. Sarah reached out her hand and put it in mine. What she couldn't communicate through signs, Sarah was very able to communicate physically. Sally called out to Jim and told him to come and see how well Sarah was responding. It would have been a huge relief for Sally, who had seen just how poorly Sarah had been. But Jim refused to come in to the sitting room, I'm not sure why. When I left the room, Jim had gone back in to see Sarah, and I heard him saying to her, "You do love daddy, don't you? You do love mummy, don't you?" He kept repeating this, over and over again.

My dad also called by to say hello to Sarah a little later on. Although he was not generally confident being around children like Sarah, he too had spent quite a bit of time with her thanks to my involvement with the children – he and my mum had even accompanied us on several days out. He came home with rather an anxious expression on his face.

He recounted what he had heard when he had arrived. Jim had been sitting in the sitting room on his own with Sarah. He was repeating, over and over again the exact same words I had heard earlier, "You do love daddy, don't you? You do love mummy, don't you? You do love daddy, don't you? You do love mummy, don't you?" Although this did seem odd at the time, and was not something I had ever heard him say before, being as fond of them all as I was, I put Jim's behaviour down to stress and anxiety over what was happening.

Dad also told me that Jim had then taken Sarah upstairs for a bath, on his own. Again, this was quite unusual behaviour – I had never, in almost five years, known Jim give Sarah a bath. Perhaps Sarah's time in hospital, and having been so poorly, might have persuaded him to spend more time with her, even if he did find it hard. Whatever his reason, I'm sure Sarah would have appreciated this quality time with her dad.

The next day was a Sunday, which was a day that I often spent with Sally and the children. More often than not Jim was out for the whole day playing football, and we would spend the day going for walks, or sometimes going out for a drive in the car. I guess Sally enjoyed having another adult to talk to and we had become good friends over the years. As much as children are good fun to be around, their level of conversation is not always that stimulating!

This particular Sunday seemed perfectly normal. I walked from my house to theirs and knocked on the front door and let myself in, as I always did. Jim was out. I knew he would be as he had asked me the previous day what time I would be there in the morning. He had seemed relieved that I would not arrive until after he had gone out, although I wasn't sure why he had needed to know or why he would be relieved that he would not be there. Sally, Thomas and Milly were in the sitting room when I arrived and a few minutes later Sarah came in.

The moment she saw me, Sarah reacted aggressively. She was terribly upset and in a state of some anguish, making it very clear by waving her arms around and shouting that she wanted me to leave. She was inconsolable. I couldn't believe what was happening; I had never seen Sarah behave this way. Sally was visibly upset too, as were the other children. Sarah's outburst was totally out of character. There was nothing I could say or do to make things any better. I was left with no choice but to go home.

I arrived home in quite a state. Sally telephoned minutes later and asked my mum if she could pop down in order to see how Sarah reacted towards both her and me. Perhaps she was more traumatised from her stay in hospital and from being away from her home and family than any of us had realised, and this was her way of letting us know. Mum agreed and off she went, on her own to begin with. Sarah behaved completely normally with my mum but as soon as I arrived the same aggressive reaction happened again.

To this day I do not understand why Sarah reacted towards me the way she did. She had been absolutely fine with me the previous day, but overnight something had changed. Thinking about it afterwards, it felt as if something must have been said to Sarah to make her behave the way she did towards me, but what could have been said to make her so fearful of me? I really had no idea, the encounter had just felt rather staged, and was not like Sarah at all. We had always had such a lovely relationship.

Back at home, I sat at the kitchen table with my head in my hands, distraught. When I eventually pulled myself together, I sat up to listen as my parents talked about what was happening. A knowing look passed between them. They turned back towards me and mum told me that it was time to appoint a solicitor.

How ridiculous, I thought. Why on earth would I need a solicitor? I hadn't done anything wrong. Surely you only need a solicitor if you are guilty of something? I know now how very naïve I was – I had complete faith in our judicial system and the work of the various bodies employed to ensure that justice will prevail. I suppose I had never had any reason before to question the way the police, social services or any other organisation conducted themselves. Plus I was only twenty years old. And I certainly wasn't about to accept that Sally was anything other than a very dear and loyal friend, and I got on pretty well with Jim too. I was not prepared now to start believing what my parents were about to tell me.

"You're being set up," my dad stated, calmly. "You are the perfect scapegoat."

Three

My reaction was explosive. I could not believe what my dad was saying, and what both my parents clearly believed. I hated them. There was absolutely no way I was going to believe it, not in a month of Sundays.

It took a good while for me to calm down; I was not only extremely angry but quite indignant that my parents had got it wrong. I slammed a few doors on the way up to my bedroom, and slammed my bedroom door even harder. I must have sat on my bed and cried for an hour or more. What was happening? Life had been so good. How could these people invade my life, invade Sally and Jim's life, invade Sarah's life, and throw us all into such turmoil? How dare they? The whole situation was a living nightmare.

I did calm down – eventually – and really started to think about what my dad had said. It just couldn't be true. Sally and Jim weren't just my employers; they were my friends too. Did my dad really mean that he thought they were making me a scapegoat? What he was saying had to be a mistake, perhaps I had misunderstood him as there was just no way – they knew me and cared about me just as much as I cared about them.

I then started to think about the many times my parents and I had argued about the amount of time I was spending with the family, at the expense of my studies. That was it; that had to be it. This was a way for my parents to stop me spending my time with Sally and the children. They were desperate for me to knuckle down and work hard. That was their reason for saying what they had. I was no scapegoat – this was just a means to an end for my parents.

My relationship with my parents had always been good, even through my turbulent pubescent years. Of course there was the odd argument or misunderstanding along the way, but generally speaking we had always got on very well. I think my brother gave them a much harder time than I did; he was a terrible teenager and I think I learnt from his mistakes! But my good relationship with my parents changed when I had started working for Sally and Jim. When I initially went to work for them in the shop, my parents had been very supportive – and they had actively encouraged me to find some part-time work when I had finished my exams. However, as the amount of time I was spending with the family increased, it created huge tension and disagreements between us. My parents knew I had the potential to do well academically, as my exam results when I was sixteen had shown. All they wanted, I now know, was for me to achieve my potential, and there was just no way this would happen when I was spending so much of my spare time with Sally and the children. But at the time I interpreted their concern completely differently.

I told my parents in no uncertain terms that I did not want a solicitor. I did not need one – it would be a waste of money. I also told them that their scheme was not going to work. Nothing would make me stay away from Sally and the children, nothing.

I expected them to listen to what I had said, to respect my wishes and to say no more about this silly idea in their heads. But they didn't. Behind the scenes they began looking for a solicitor – they were worried for me, and convinced that I did need one. The person they found, recommended to them, was Philip Dawes. I did not find out, of course, that they had enlisted Philip Dawes until the day of my arrest. I continued to believe that the police and social workers would eventually realise that this investigation was a complete waste of time, and they would go away and let us get on with our lives. It was surely just a matter of time, and that I had plenty of...

After this awful encounter with Sarah, and with what my parents were saying going round and round in my head, I stopped seeing as much of Sally and the children, not least because Sally didn't ask me to help out any more. I did call in to the house a few more times, but things had changed. I was devastated that Sarah had behaved the way she had towards me, of course, but more than that I felt completely bemused by her behaviour. I could not think of anything that might have triggered her aggression. It was so totally out of character. What could possibly have influenced her to behave so strangely?

Little did I know until much further down the line that Sally and Jim reported this incident to the police the following day. I suppose they must have felt that it had some significance to their investigation. I can only think now, looking back, that they felt it implicated me.

Again, I had no idea at the time, but my parents also

reported the same incident to the police. When we talked about it some months later, they told me their firm belief that this situation had been staged, that something must have been said to Sarah in order to make her behave this way towards me, probably without understanding what she was doing or at least what her behaviour seemed to imply.

In total I saw the children three or four more times, usually calling in on my way home from college. Sarah didn't ever react in that violently negative way towards me again, but that didn't make any difference whatsoever; I still wasn't made to feel particularly welcome, even though Sally always said her usual, "See you later" when I left to go home. I hoped so much that this meant she did want me to carry on spending time with them all, but looking back I think her attitude towards me reflected more accurately her feelings towards me. I think she was trying, or had possibly even been advised, to keep things as normal as possible, which is probably why she didn't ever tell me I wasn't welcome in her home anymore and why she always said, "See you later". However, the reality was that this situation was far from normal, and there is no doubt in my mind now that the last thing she wanted was me turning up to see them all, especially the children. She must have found it virtually impossible to continue being nice to me when it would appear the idea that I was the alleged abuser had already surfaced. On the other hand, despite my parents having voiced their concerns, I remained adamant that they were wrong, and was desperately clinging on to the hope that everything would work out and that my friendship with Sally and my relationship with the children would eventually get back to normal.

How I managed I don't know, but I carried on working

in the shop for a few more weeks. Things felt very different though. Sally had in the past always made a point of calling in to see how my morning or afternoon was going, and to make me a cup of tea, but now I rarely saw her, other than at closing time to hand the till over. There was a terrible atmosphere between us – things had changed, but I knew that the situation with Sarah was causing untold stress. She didn't want to talk to me, that much was clear.

And things were much the same with Jim. I hadn't ever got to know him particularly well, despite the fact that I had spent much time in his company; I wasn't sure if he was shy or just a very quiet person but he certainly wasn't an easy person to get to know. We'd had conversations over the years but we had nothing in common, and if I'm honest I struggled to understand the way he treated Sarah and felt myself constantly biting my tongue in order not to say anything to him about it. I felt very sorry for Sarah, and worried that she might feel sad about her dad too.

But by now I was hurting so badly. I didn't know how to deal with my feelings at all, they were so intense. I felt an incredible loss, both of Sarah and the rest of the family; I think I had become as dependent on them as they were on me. Some evenings I would walk to our local pub and have a few strong drinks to try to numb the pain; but they didn't make any difference, other than causing me to be very sick! I didn't want to talk to anybody; this wasn't the kind of thing you would open up to people about over a drink, but I didn't think anyone would understand how I was feeling anyway. All I wanted was to take the pain away. Sally and her family were going through hell, and I was being pushed away rather than being allowed to offer them support. If I wasn't in the pub I would talk to friends on the telephone, mainly Laura and Martha, but at this point I don't think any of us appreciated the severity of the situation or indeed the course of events that would follow.

The following Saturday afternoon I was working in the shop and Sally, obviously in a bad mood, started to say some particularly cruel things to me. I suppose I could defend her and say that she must have been under a huge amount of stress at that time, but by this point I had had enough – I just couldn't take any more, and I certainly couldn't cope with her unkindness. So I left work early, walking home in tears once more.

By the time I reached home, Sally had telephoned my parents and been rude to them as well. She had asked for some of the children's toys that had been left at our house to be returned, and my mum had suggested she should call at the house to collect them. She eventually turned up at the house a while later and for some reason continued with her rudeness. Before leaving with the toys she had come for, Sally went on to ask me for the sign language booklet I had. She didn't try to give any explanation for wanting the booklet. She just kept repeating that she wanted it back. I had attended a few Makaton classes to try to always keep one step ahead of what Sarah was learning, and the booklet I had was actually photocopied material that had been given to me at the classes and did not belong to Sally at all; but she was absolutely adamant that I should hand it over to her. I did not give her the booklet, and I remember that this fuelled her anger even more. I really couldn't understand why she was making so much fuss; she would have had her own copy of exactly the same material, so why the need to take mine from me?

While she was at our house Sally also told us that she

was no longer permitted to leave Sarah on her own with other adults. We later found out that this was untrue and Sally appeared to have said it simply to make sure I knew that I would never again be left on my own with Sarah. Who had made the decision to tell me that I do not know, but it was devastating to hear, not least because it confirmed to us all that I really was a suspect in this dreadful investigation, even if only in the eyes of Sally and perhaps Jim too. For me this realisation was more than I could cope with but it was no longer possible to deny what was happening right in front of our eyes.

Sally also told us that Sarah was going into hospital the following week for a serious operation. The alleged abuse that she had been subjected to had apparently caused such severe constipation that she was vomiting faeces and as a result she needed urgent surgery. Sally told us that she was likely to be in hospital for around a week.

Sally left our house eventually; as a parting shot she told my parents how fond of me she was and that I was a wonderful person. But I didn't believe her anymore. Her words were empty, meaningless even. I felt totally overwhelmed with this whole situation, and no longer knew where I stood. Sally was fond of me yet at the same time didn't seem to want me around her children; nothing was making any sense.

But that didn't really matter anymore; all I could think about was Sarah and everything that was happening to her. I wanted to give her a big cuddle and tell her that it would all be OK, but I now knew in my heart of hearts that I would never see her again.

I was terribly worried about the surgery that Sarah was about to have, and on the day of the operation asked my dad to call in to see Sally or Jim and find out if she was all right. I had no intention of visiting her in the hospital – that would be inappropriate, I knew – but I still needed to know that she was OK.

Dad spoke to Jim and was told that Sarah was fine, she was home, and would probably be returning to school the next day. That was great news. I was so relieved but at the same time somewhat taken aback, as Sally had implied that the operation Sarah would be having was quite major. I had understood that she would be in hospital for about a week, if not longer.

All of these events, from Sarah being admitted to hospital right through to the point when I was arrested, took place over a period of around six weeks, but it really did feel like a lifetime. I did not work in the shop during the two weeks leading up to my arrest, and I did not see the children either.

I had spent the previous four or five years believing that I had a genuinely good working relationship with Sally and Jim, and Sally especially had also become a firm friend. The stern exterior I had been so scared of at first had softened over time and I had found her to be a kind and caring person. I felt that both she and Jim had always shown an interest in my studies and had offered help and support if needed, although my parents would of course argue that it would have been in my best interests if they had encouraged me to study more and spend less time with them. In return I had been nothing but loyal and hard-working, almost at the expense of my own personal life. The reality, I now realised, was so different. I had been convenient at the time, an extra pair of hands, somebody who could actually be easily disposed of if need be, and this was exactly what was happening right now.

All confidence I had had in myself had disappeared and I even questioned my ability to do anything other than the mundane job of helping look after somebody else's children. My relationship with my parents had been put under considerable strain too. My early teenage years had been filled with hopes and dreams of a high-flying career, getting married and having my own children – yet somehow these hopes and dreams had all but vanished. I had, without realising it, given up pretty much everything I had ever strived for. I had completely lost my way during the past years.

But I had to start facing up to the reality of this situation, that much was true. What my dad had said at the outset was true: Sally and Jim had now closed ranks, turned their backs on me and it seemed they had also turned against me. There had been no explanation, no goodbyes, nothing. From where I was standing and from where my parents were standing, it did seem that I was no longer the much thought of and greatly appreciated friend and employee, and this was an incredibly hard realisation to accept.

Around two weeks after Sarah came out of hospital following her UTI, the social worker who had been assigned to the investigation contacted my parents and requested a meeting at our house. We had no reason at all to refuse this meeting, even though we were unsure of its exact purpose. Perhaps he too thought that a friendly informal chat might encourage me to say something that would consequently help him or the police to discover what had happened to Sarah. But my experiences to date were suggesting to me that perhaps he thought I might trip myself up and end up implicating myself. But of course this would not happen as I had nothing to hide. I knew nothing, and could not tell him anything other than the fact that I had never had cause to worry about any of the individuals who looked after Sarah. I would just be completely honest with him.

My preconception of a social worker, probably thanks to some programme or other that I had seen on television, was of a youngish hippy type with long hair, whether male or female, and dangly earrings (probably more earring holes than the conventional one in each ear), wearing sandals and very bright, flowing clothes. However, Mr Smith was nothing like this. He was a small man with not much hair. He was quite old – in fact I am sure he must have been reaching retirement. And he wore a smart (ish) suit. There were no earrings, either!

This first meeting with Mr Smith took place at our house. My parents were out at work and at this point I guess they were not concerned enough to feel the need to be present. Mr Smith was in fact going through a process of familiarising himself with everyone involved with Sarah's care, we assumed.

Mr Smith began by commenting on our wallpaper – how pretty it was! After this – and in fact our wallpaper was actually fairly old and in need of freshening up – he asked me who I thought might be responsible for abusing Sarah. I responded just as I had to the police officers at the hospital – I had no idea. I still didn't want to believe that she had been abused. I couldn't come to terms at all with this idea, so I found it virtually impossible to start looking at anyone as a potential abuser. These people, Sally, Jim, the children's grandparents, aunts, uncles and cousins, staff from Sarah's school, they were all my friends, I had spent time with many of them socially. Did Mr Smith, or anybody else for that matter, really expect me to start pointing the finger at any one of these people? There was just no way, and I certainly would never have pointed the finger unless I had anything specific to report. All I could do was tell the truth as I knew it.

I had by now had a lot of time to think and to reflect on the previous five years. I had been a very naïve teenager, admittedly, but sexual abuse was not something that I had ever thought about, not just as far as Sarah was concerned, but ever. OK, I didn't suspect, during the time I was working for her parents, that she had been abused, but would anyone have done so? Why would anyone automatically assume, if a child was upset or if their behaviour was a little different, that they were being abused? One million and one other causes would spring to mind first, surely? They certainly would have done as far as I was concerned.

I mentioned earlier a day trip when Sarah had seemed subdued, and had wet her pants twice. Articles and books about abuse will often tell you that either of these symptoms can be indicative of sexual abuse. I know quite a lot about this subject now – I have done a lot of reading about child abuse since the investigation – at the time I had no idea. I merely assumed that she was coming down with something, and would probably have a stinker of a cold within the next day or two. I do feel sad that there might have been more to Sarah's behaviour than I realised that day, but this was an isolated incident and there was just no way that I could ever have been expected to interpret things any other way.

I explained all of this to Mr Smith during his visit, but the events that ensued left me only able to believe that everything I said had fallen on deaf ears.

Around four weeks after the meeting with Mr Smith came the day of my arrest.

Four

The police had arrived at our house, and I was to be taken to the local police station for questioning. My mum, absolutely furious, asked the officers to wait while she telephoned Philip Dawes, the solicitor my parents had appointed behind my back. But they refused to do this. For what seemed like hours but was probably just a few minutes, I was rooted to the spot on the doorstep, completely numb with shock. Mum knew that Philip Dawes had spoken to the police officers involved in the investigation some weeks earlier, and they had agreed that, should they need to talk to me, they would contact him so that he could in turn contact me and arrange to accompany me to the police station for questioning, hence her reason for being angry with them. As I was still studying some sixty miles away, and usually only at home in the evenings, Philip Dawes had felt this arrangement would make it easier for everyone involved, not least himself as he wanted to make sure he would be available to attend any proposed interviews.

But that was not to be, and my mum was absolutely livid. She confronted the officers, and was told by the detective sergeant that he had been informed I was about to leave the area, hence their decision to arrest me rather than adhere to what had previously been agreed. It turned out, we were informed at a later date, it was Sally who had contacted the police and told them she understood that I was about to leave the area. Where I was supposed to be about to go I have no idea; apart from anything else this was all happening right in the middle of my university term! And more importantly, I had no reason whatsoever to want to leave the area; I was completely innocent and had nothing to run away from. I would cooperate with any part of the investigation. I really couldn't understand why Sally would have told the police something she knew to be untrue.

Mum then asked to be allowed to accompany me to the police station in their car, but she was told that their insurance would not cover her! This, it later turned out, was also untrue. It was their way of intimidating me – or so they thought. By this time I had thankfully rediscovered some of my old inner strength, and nobody was going to frighten me into admitting something that was just not true. I would fight with every ounce of strength I could summon.

Before I was led away (thankfully not handcuffed; that would have been the last straw for my poor mum) I telephoned my friend Martha. I had confided in her from the start, and she immediately came up to the house, arriving just as I was being driven away. At least she might be able to support mum, I thought. My dad was still at work and I wasn't sure whether mum would manage to get hold of him as he had been away from the office for the day, in meetings somewhere way up north, and he might not be contactable. I was worried that the strain of this situation might take its toll on mum; her health had been quite poor for some years and I was sure that this wouldn't help her one bit.

In the event, one of mum and dad's closest and oldest friends came and met my mum at the police station, so that at least she would not have to wait there on her own.

The drive to the police station was strange. The WPC did try to start up a conversation with me a couple of times, but I sat in silence. Mum had instructed me not to say a word until I was at the station and with my solicitor, but I wouldn't have spoken to them anyway. Just before we arrived at the station, the WPC explained what would happen as soon as we got there; she told me that it would be similar to the television programme The Bill, which I was familiar with.

The first few minutes at the police station were a blur. I do remember that it was a hive of activity, and I seemed to be one of several arrestees being dealt with. I was asked to remove any jewellery I was wearing. I assumed from this (and from what I had seen on The Bill) that I was going to be put in a cell, and I probably would have been if my solicitor had not arrived at that exact moment.

We were put in a small room and given a few minutes to acquaint ourselves. I remember vividly the smell of pipe smoke – Philip Dawes had a pipe sticking out of his mouth throughout and was puffing on it gently. These were the days when smoking was still permitted anywhere and everywhere. I found the smell rather pleasant; it reminded me a little of my dad, as he was a cigar smoker, but pipe smoke was a far nicer smell, I had always thought. Philip Dawes didn't really try to advise me, other than to say that he would speak up if anything inappropriate was asked of me. And that was fine. I had every intention of cooperating with the police; I knew that I had done nothing wrong, and naturally assumed that they would therefore believe me.

I still at this time had a naïve belief that justice would prevail.

It was early evening when the interview began, and it lasted around two hours; I hadn't eaten before the police had arrived at my house to arrest me and I was hungry, my tummy was rumbling too. The same two police officers who had come to the house and taken me to the station carried out the questioning, and it was very clear from the outset that they were going to play the 'good cop, bad cop' routine. I had seen this way of interviewing on television too, so at least it didn't come as a complete surprise!

It turned out that Sarah had been interviewed by the police a couple of weeks earlier. They had in fact had to interview her twice, as the first interview was unsuccessful. Or in other words, in my opinion, she did not give them the responses they had hoped for. My view of the police here is not, I know, a particularly positive one – but it was now becoming obvious to me that rather than working to determine exactly what had or had not happened to Sarah, they were going to treat the situation as if she had been abused and they therefore needed to find the evidence to confirm this.

The evidence put forward at my interview by the police came from the examination carried out by the paediatrician at the hospital, in which he had discovered possible physical signs of sexual abuse, and also from the interview with Sarah.

According to the police, the paediatrician had ruled out the possibility that Sarah could have hurt herself, and it was also considered unlikely that the physical evidence could be linked with her disabilities. I don't know exactly how these options were ruled out, but this was what I was told. The officers also stated that the paediatrician believed Sarah to almost certainly have been abused, stating a 90% certainty.

This last statement we later found out to be untrue; there was absolutely no certainty that she had been abused. The police also claimed during my interview that Sarah had been abused by somebody over the age of fourteen, but we later found out that it would actually have been impossible to establish the age of the alleged abuser. I was also told that the alleged abuse had taken place during a period of approximately five years. This statement also lacked credence, we later found out.

During the investigation the officers seemed to be bandying about several accounts of the alleged abuse, and it was difficult to be certain which was the correct one. Not only did the degree of certainty that Sarah had been abused differ depending on who you were talking to, but the period over which the alleged abuse was supposed to have occurred differed too.

I was shown two clips of the interview with Sarah. Interestingly, her siblings had also been interviewed, and had not said anything to give any cause for concern. In the clips of Sarah, she was being interviewed by the female WPC, and was accompanied by her mother, who was also doing any necessary interpretation. Sarah was using her talking machine – this was a very new part of her life, and was basically a screen full of pictures and photographs, which when pressed spoke what was in the picture. She had only started using the machine a month or two before she had been admitted to hospital, and so only had a small number of pictures on it, probably half a dozen or so, and just two photographs. The first two photographs that were put on the machine were of her school bus driver and the helper on the bus. In time I believe it was planned to add photographs of everyone who played a part in Sarah's life, but when she was admitted to hospital there were still just the two photographs.

However, by the time of this interview, my photograph had also been added.

Sarah was asked by the police officer, "Who hurts Sarah? Tell me. Someone on there?" She pointed to Sarah's machine. Sarah's response was to press the photograph of me and put her hands between her legs.

Sarah only had three people to choose from. What if she had indeed been abused but by somebody else, how would she would have been able to indicate this to the police officer? The way the question was asked appeared to suggest to Sarah that she needed to choose one of us three, regardless of what the reality was, even if she had in fact not been abused at all. It would surely be deemed a leading question. Significantly, too, the officer had not used any signs to make sure that she was communicating completely clearly what she was asking, and it would be impossible to know whether Sarah had understood the question.

Sadly though, as far as the police were concerned that did not matter and Sarah's response was cut and dried. I had abused Sarah, they decided, because this was what she had communicated to them. I had to agree that Sarah's response could be seen as telling them this, but I tried to explain that it could also have meant a number of other things. I knew that Sarah would put her hands between her legs when she was constipated. What she was trying to express when the police asked her this question, I really had no idea, but her response was not dissimilar to that movement. I repeated the concern that my parents had expressed, and which I had now started to realise myself – that perhaps Sarah was being primed and almost taught to react the way she did each time my name was mentioned; in the same way she may have been encouraged to react aggressively towards me when I had called at the house several weeks earlier. But again I'm not sure that my response was really listened to.

It wasn't until after my interview, when I had time to reflect upon what I had seen in the clips, that my concerns about what was happening grew even more. I worried about how the police officer did not use signs to communicate with Sarah, only spoke to her – to the best of my knowledge there was no sign for "hurt", but even if there had been, how on earth would Sarah be able to know that the word "hurt" was in this context to mean "abuse"? Also, where Sarah responded with signs rather than her machine, it was her mum who interpreted these signs for the police. I had never ever seen Sarah communicate by putting two signs together – the fact that she had pressed my photograph and then put her hands between her legs suggested to me that she had very quickly learnt this new skill, but I found this hard to believe. Sarah just would not have had the ability to progress so swiftly.

The second clip I saw had shown Sarah continually pressing my photograph on her machine and then swiping her finger across her eye. Sally told the police officer that this meant I was crying. My interpretation, in hindsight, would have been that Sarah wanted to see me, but I could not remember this particular sign during the interview. "To cry" and "to see" are not dissimilar signs, and Sarah's accuracy was not great, leaving much room for interpretation. Here too she was also putting two signs together, which as I said was very new and more advanced than I had thought she was – whenever I had been with her she had only ever used a single sign or a single button on her machine. The police, however, seemed more than happy to accept her mother's interpretation of what Sarah was communicating.

Surely, surely, Sally's interpretation of these signs should have been queried? Or, even if Sally had been allowed to stay in the room with Sarah in order to reassure her, there would be an independent person outside the room who could verify what Sarah was communicating? While the signs are all unique, anybody using them would need a certain degree of accuracy, which Sarah did not yet have – I had spent a great deal of time with her, much more than the police had, and there had been numerous times in the past when even I had had difficulty understanding what she was trying to tell me. With an independent person, there could still have been some uncertainty about trying to interpret what Sarah was communicating, but at least there would not have been any bias. I am unsure whether an interpreter was involved in Sarah's interview, but I do hope there was.

The previous six weeks had seen Sally and Jim turn their backs on me completely and seemingly manipulate situations and events that in turn helped to persuade the police of my guilt. So I wasn't very surprised, really, that the same appeared to have happened at Sarah's interview, in that Sally was the main interpreter of what Sarah was trying to communicate. It was another tool that might enable them to create more doubt about my innocence.

There was just nothing I could say to the police to make them believe that I had not harmed Sarah. I didn't even know exactly what I was supposed to have done; and all they seemed to be able to tell me was that somebody had interfered with her down below (although the paediatrician had been definite, thankfully, that she had not been raped). She was sore and there was some scarring. There was no way of proving my innocence, especially as I had obviously had the opportunity to harm her had I wanted to. I had bathed all of the children at one time or another, and had been on my own with all of them on multiple occasions. I did tell the police that I felt Sarah, who was quite strong physically, and quite a large girl, would put up a fight if something had been happening that she didn't want to happen. As an adult I was obviously larger and stronger than Sarah, but if I had tried to do something to her that she objected to, I truly believe she would have fought against me and made a lot of noise doing so. Aggressive outbursts, although not frequent, did happen from time to time, and often for quite mundane reasons such as not wanting to do something she had been asked to do. Surely therefore she would have reacted as aggressively if not more so, if somebody tried to hurt her. There were often people around, if not actually in the same room as us in the next room, or upstairs. It would just not have been possible without somebody hearing a commotion. The times that I was alone with Sarah, with nobody else within earshot, were not that frequent.

There were no specific dates or times given either, otherwise I might have been able to prove that I had not been with Sarah when the abuse was supposed to have taken place. As I said previously, there were several versions given of the details of the abuse and each person or organisation involved in the investigation reported slightly differing accounts: one that the abuse had taken place over an eighteen-month period, another that it had taken place over five years... Whether or not an accurate timescale was ever established I do not know, but the inference was certainly that the alleged abuse coincided with the time I had spent working for the family.

I cared, obviously, about Sally and the children, having known them now for several years, and it was just beyond my belief that this was happening. Even though Sally had been rejecting my help ever since Sarah's hospitalisation, the kind things she had said and done over the years kept coming back to me, and I couldn't bring myself to turn against her. She had told me at first that she knew I hadn't hurt Sarah, so why did she now seem to believe it? I guess the saying "blood is thicker than water" is true and when it came down to it, I wasn't a relative, and therefore could be disposed of very easily.

The police wanted to discuss the conversation I had had in the hospital canteen with Sally. Why had I said that I wanted to wrap Sarah up and bring her home? Was this because I had abused her and wanted to stop anybody discovering the truth? What? No! I told them so, and that I had actually meant I wanted to protect Sarah from this horrible situation and take her home to normality.

But it really didn't matter what I had meant; they were going to use my comments completely out of context, and of course Sally hadn't mentioned the other part of this conversation, in which she told me she knew that I would not have harmed Sarah.

The police were also interested in my personal life, and boyfriends in particular. At that time I did not have a boyfriend, although I had recently been involved with a young man for a year or so. He was also a university student and we had been introduced by mutual friends. We did get on very well, but I certainly wasn't ready for anything serious and I don't think he was either. Apart from anything else, we were both studying in different places and only saw each other during the holidays. He was a really lovely person, but the fact that I have not mentioned him until this point in the book probably tells you that he was never going to be more than just a very dear friend. And we did remain friends for a couple of years after the relationship ended. He had met Sarah a few times, too, and had come out with us on one of our day trips. For the police, however, the fact that I was a single woman seemed to give them even more reason to question the propriety of my relationship with Sarah. How ridiculous. I could not believe what I was hearing. How could the times I had shared with Sarah, and her siblings for that matter, be interpreted as anything other than what they were – fun; innocent fun.

As the interview drew to a close, I was feeling extremely confused by what I was hearing and very frustrated that there just seemed to be no way I could prove I had done nothing wrong. The police commented that I had appeared very calm throughout the interview, again implying, I thought, that this somehow indicated guilt. I certainly hadn't felt calm inside, but I also had no intention of being cajoled into saying anything other than what I knew to be the truth.

It seemed that I had to defend myself against Sarah's entire family now too; I had assumed, wrongly, that they would support me as they were supporting each other through the knowledge that Sarah had apparently been abused under our very noses. How wrong I was. The truth of the matter was that there was no way I would even be sitting here being interviewed if they had portrayed me and my relationship with Sarah accurately to the police. And why had they allowed me to look after any of their children for almost five years, if they had any doubts about my integrity? It didn't make sense. Why hadn't they wanted to sit down and talk to me about what was happening, to pool our thoughts about what might or might not have happened to Sarah? Had any of us ever had any concerns about anything or anyone who came in to contact with Sarah? Had any of us ever seen her playing with herself? Could the symptoms have been caused by her constipation? We hadn't ever had that conversation; almost from day one Sally and Jim had seemed intent on pointing the finger at me, but why?

If Sarah had been my child, I am certain that as a parent I would have wanted every avenue explored; I would not have readily accepted that my child had been abused unless the evidence suggesting so was as conclusive as it could be; in this case it certainly was not conclusive. I would have wanted to know what else, if anything, might have caused the physical signs of abuse. I would also have insisted that absolutely everybody who had come into contact with my child was investigated.

At a later date my parents talked to a relative who had spent years working with adults who had mental and physical disabilities, and her experience told her that those adults who suffered from chronic constipation, like Sarah, did sometimes display the scarring and soreness that Sarah had, as a result. I too had of course made the point about constipation to the police, but it seemed that they hadn't taken it on board at all.

This just didn't seem to interest Sally and Jim either; from where I was standing they appeared to have readily accepted the notion that their daughter had been abused. And by now they seemed to be using every opportunity they had to tell everybody they knew – friends, family, customers – what was happening, including the fact that I was the primary suspect. What I could not comprehend was their reason for pointing the finger of blame at me. They knew, without any shadow of a doubt, that I would never have hurt Sarah.

That question will haunt me until the day I die.

Five

I was released by the police and requested to return to the station four weeks later. Both of my parents were waiting at the station, along with their friend.

The police explained that they planned to send their 'evidence' to the Crown Prosecution Service (CPS), and that the CPS would make the decision as to whether I would be charged with the alleged offence. So there would be a long wait, but it didn't really cross my mind that I would be charged – there would surely need to be more evidence than there was? My solicitor Philip Dawes, who had spoken very little throughout, continued to puff on his pipe as we parted ways. He was, he said, contactable if I had any questions or concerns; otherwise he would see me at the station in four weeks' time.

That evening we sat at home, much of the time in silence. We were all thinking about what had happened, trying to understand why it had happened, and my parents, being ever practical, trying to decide how best to deal with what was being thrown our way. I don't think any decisions were made that evening, I certainly wasn't in any fit state to do anything and I'm sure my dad had more than one glass of whisky! All I really wanted to do was knock on Sally and Jim's front door and ask them if they had any idea what they were doing to me. I didn't only feel let down, I felt completely used, and actually pretty worthless now that they had washed their hands of me. I felt that I had been left to drown. Not only that but they were pointing the finger of blame at me, albeit in a rather subtle way. For all I knew, though, they may have told all sorts of made up stories to the police, hoping that this would lead them to believe I was guilty. I would of course never know what was said, or more importantly to me at the time, what on earth had led them to behave this way.

I have no idea how, but somehow I returned to university the following day, determined to carry on with life as normal. But of course it was far from normal. My whole world had changed; I no longer had Sally and the children to call in on after university, or to spend time with at weekends. I needed somehow to reacquaint myself with my parents, who I had neglected badly over the past five years or so. I felt very lonely all of a sudden, and realised that the life I had been leading had not actually been my life at all; it was Sally and Jim's life and I had been a helping hand while convenient. Now I was no longer useful to them, I realised, my own life had slowly fallen down around my ears without me even noticing. My parents had put up with so much, and my friendships had suffered. How had I allowed this situation to happen, and worse still how had I not noticed? Sally and Jim must have had such a strong hold on me, without me even realising; I had been there, at their beck and call, at the expense of everything and everyone else. And now I had to hold my hands up and try to make things right, first of all with my parents and then with my friends.

But actually this turned out to be much easier than expected. All anyone wanted was to see me from time to time, to spend some quality time with me, and for me not to be always rushing off to help with the children. And time was something that I suddenly had lots of. So very quickly my relationship with my parents was back on track and friends were telephoning once more, asking if I wanted to go out and do things that normal young people would do, but which I hadn't done much of for quite some time.

Thank goodness my parents and friends were back in my life, as I was discovering that I needed a great deal of emotional support. This whole situation had already had, and would continue for many years to have, a massive impact on me. My emotions were all over the place. I felt such incredible loss, especially as far as Sally and Sarah were concerned. I cared about the entire family, of course, but these two had a particularly special place in my heart. I had thought of Sally as a dear friend, and Sarah as a kid sister I suppose, and it was almost like grieving for people who had died, as I knew I would never see them again. I was also now starting to feel anger though, towards both Sally and Jim but especially Jim – I felt that it was he who had done what he could to point the finger at me. I had, after all, heard him with my own ears telling the police officer that I was behaving in a guilty manner. But then it had been Sally who had contacted the police and told them I was about to leave the area, and it was this call that had prompted my arrest. Perhaps she too was pointing the finger at me, but I was just not ready to believe this yet. I kept fighting off these feelings of anger as much as I could, but it really was only going to be a matter of time before they got the better of me.

At some point between my arrest and discovering the outcome from the CPS, Philip Dawes contacted the social services solicitor to discuss the case. During their conversation the solicitor stated categorically that there was no certainty Sarah had been abused, and that if the police had stated this during my interview, it was untrue. The police had in fact said that there was a 90% certainty; where they had obtained this figure I do not know.

Also between my arrest and discovering the outcome from the CPS, Philip Dawes bumped in to one of the police officers involved in this case; they had been attending the same court. Philip Dawes expressed his concern to the officer about the possible misinterpretation of Sarah's signs by Sally during her interview, stating that he was not surprised this might have happened. Before parting company, the officer referred back to Sally's interpretation of one sign meaning "to cry" rather than "to see." It was reassuring at least to know that Philip Dawes had had the opportunity to raise this as a concern.

Although I had been asked to go back to the police station four weeks after my arrest, it actually didn't take quite that long for the CPS to decide that I would not be charged. Two days before I was due at the police station I received a letter saying, "Based on the evidence revealed by the investigation to date, it is not proposed to institute proceedings against you." More significantly, we were later informed their written advice to the police had stated that, "There is no evidence that any offence has been committed by anyone, let alone Jessie Kyd."

Even though I had not believed for one moment that I would be charged, I am the first to admit that it was a relief to see it confirmed in writing. And it would be even better if I could now report that this whole sorry episode was well and truly over and that I was able to start picking up the pieces of my life and could try to get back to some kind of normality.

Sadly, though, the police investigation was just the tip of the iceberg. I had already been made aware that the social services were not going to let this case drop and had planned a meeting to discuss the situation, scheduled to take place approximately two weeks after my arrest, at the beginning of December, and before the CPS would have reached their decision.

My solicitor explained that the police and social services work on different levels of proof – police need evidence that proves an individual's guilt beyond reasonable doubt, while the social services base their evidence on the balance of probability. These are, it turns out, significantly different, in that a much lower level of proof is needed by the social services. The social services can do their investigative work with much less evidence, enabling them to make decisions with a lesser degree of certainty. The fact that I would not be charged by the police would be irrelevant as far as they were concerned.

I was devastated by this. I had had no idea that social workers had this kind of authority.

This meeting was what they called a case conference, designed to make decisions primarily about the child involved, in this instance Sarah, and what measures if any needed to be put in place in order to ensure her safety and well-being in the future. In addition to these decisions about Sarah, in this instance social services were also proposing to discuss the fact that I was currently training to be a teacher. They felt that they needed to discuss whether or not my university should be informed that I was a suspect in the abuse investigation. I could not believe that they had the right to make this sort of decision – it could potentially have a drastic and very negative impact on my life.

Philip Dawes and I were initially invited to attend the case conference, but just a few days beforehand the invitation was overturned. It was a surprising and disappointing blow and we were never entirely clear why I was not permitted to attend. I thought perhaps some of those attending might feel uncomfortable discussing me if I was present at the meeting, but this was just a thought. Philip Dawes was extremely efficient, though, and between us we prepared a lengthy document outlining everything that we considered relevant and that might help my case. The document provided a brief overview of my life and my current studies but focussed primarily on the years I had spent working for Sally and her family. It was my opportunity in some ways to try to prove my innocence, I suppose, but how you could possibly hope to do this without knowing exactly what was supposed to have happened to Sarah, I am not sure. All I could realistically hope to do was show the panel that I was a normal, kind and caring human being. I firmly believe that the panel would have got to know me better had I been allowed to attend and I can only hope that this document was read out or at least given to everybody attending the meeting, with the intention that they would read it.

We were told afterwards by the social worker Mr Smith, with whom we had had a previous meeting, the names of the people who had been present at the meeting; I don't think we would ever have known otherwise. As well as social workers these included Sarah's headteacher and class teacher, the WPC involved in the case and also Sally and

Jim. Their GP, who was a GP at the surgery we also used, was there. The paediatrician who saw Sarah in hospital did not attend the meeting.

I always felt that our GP should have declined the invitation to attend. One of the families, either mine or Sally's, would inevitably, surely, end up feeling that he had taken sides, if he was to be involved in any decision making. The case conference was going to make decisions about ensuring Sarah's ongoing safety, but it was also going to decide whether to inform my university about the allegation. Perhaps he had no choice but to attend, but nevertheless I did feel that it was wrong.

The two teachers were obviously people already involved in Sarah's life, and therefore in Sally and Jim's too. Sally was a governor at Sarah's school and she had previously told me that she had supported the school financially from time to time. I did not believe for one minute that these people would do or say anything that jeopardised the relationship they had with Sarah's family, but perhaps this was just me being sceptical. They knew me, but not well. I had spent time at the school helping with some of the children, and I hoped so much that this would be enough to reassure them that I was not the person I was now being portrayed as.

It is important to point out here that there are three individuals I am aware of who, because they knew my mum through work, were not permitted to attend the meeting. My mum had a part-time clerical job, working for the health service, and she had met all three individuals as a result of working there. They each held various senior positions within the medical profession. Had any of these people attended the meeting, they would have been representing their profession – they did not know me personally. I believe that they would have been more than appropriate independent adults, but they were all unfortunately prevented from attending because they knew my mum.

All of these other adults, who knew Sally and the children socially or professionally, were by contrast permitted to attend. At the time I thought that this was very one-sided, and looking back now I still believe this – why were none of these three individuals allowed to attend while other, possibly less independent, people were? I had no representation other than a written report. Can it really be said that whatever decision would be reached was going to be balanced and fair?

I was never informed of the outcome of the meeting as far as Sarah was concerned, and the decision about informing my university was frustratingly not made at this meeting, perhaps because no decision had yet been made by the CPS. This part of the case conference was adjourned and scheduled to take place approximately three weeks after the date when I would find out whether or not charges would be brought against me. I was faced with yet more waiting.

I assumed, naturally, once I'd had the letter saying the decision had been made not to charge me, that this meeting would not need to take place, but I was wrong.

I cannot remember anything at all about Christmas that year. I have no memory of anywhere we went, anything we did, anyone we saw, and looking through my numerous photograph albums there are none at all from that Christmas. I was known for my love of taking photographs; my camera was never far from my side, so the lack of any that Christmas must mean that it wasn't a particularly jolly one. Unsurprisingly, I guess, there was nothing to feel positive about and we were still waiting for the second meeting to take place early in the new year.

My solicitor and I were not invited to attend the reconvened meeting either. We therefore had to rely, once more, on providing a written report for those attending. I was pretty cross about not being permitted to attend; it is much easier to get points across by talking face to face and far easier for misunderstandings to arise if something presented only in writing is misinterpreted. But there was nothing we could do. Bizarrely, according to the social worker dealing with this case I had no automatic right to attend, even though the sole purpose of the meeting was to make a decision that would potentially affect the rest of my life.

We were informed that this meeting, to decide on my future, would consist of the same people who had attended the first one, which worried me hugely; I was sure that not one of these people would have my interests uppermost in their minds, but had to hope that they had read the report that Philip Dawes and I had prepared, and that this would be sufficient. We would never know. At least Sally and Jim would not be attending this meeting, but even that did not offer me any reassurances. It still seemed so one-sided, and I was feeling before the meeting even took place that the decision had probably already been made. What reason would they have for deciding not to inform the university? As far as I was aware there were no other suspects in this case, and I didn't know how the police were going to present their 'evidence'; as far as I was concerned that could well influence the meeting to believe that I had harmed Sarah.

The day of the meeting arrived and I was, needless to say, extremely anxious. I had resigned myself to the likelihood that the decision to tell my university was the inevitable outcome.

What these people did not know was that I had already, against the advice of my solicitor, talked to my tutor at university about what was happening. Philip Dawes had thought that my tutor might be under some obligation to report the matter to somebody more senior, and felt it unnecessary until we knew the CPS's decision.

But I am nothing if not honest, and attending university each day, knowing what was happening in my personal life and the impact it might have on my continuing studies, felt wrong to me. I felt as if I was being deceptive, especially as I had by now confided in my closest friends there and we were spending much of our free time talking about the situation. They had all met Sarah in the past too; I had brought her in to university two or three times. The staff there were very relaxed, and Sarah had loved it. She had been the centre of attention and thrived on it! My tutor was a nice woman who had been assigned to me on the day I started at university; she was my lecturer for some subjects as well as my personal tutor, appointed to help with the pastoral side of things.

She realised early on that something was wrong; my concentration in lessons was becoming a real issue and my attendance also dropped. There were some days when I just couldn't face getting out of bed, especially when I had begun to realise that the finger was being pointed at me. In the end I knocked on her door one day and sat down and told her everything that was happening. I had been arrested by this point, and the situation was potentially serious; whatever the outcome, it would affect me forever more.

My tutor was amazingly supportive. We both knew that there was nothing practical she could do to help, but knowing that she was there for support was a comfort.

I suspected, having been advised by my solicitor, that she would be obliged to report what I had told her to somebody in a higher position at the university, but that was something she would know how to deal with and I had to let her get on with it. It was a risk I was willing to take; I couldn't carry on with my studies unless the situation was out in the open. I told my parents that I had talked to my tutor, and my mum then made contact with her once or twice too; I think this helped the whole situation and meant that mum could contact her if I was feeling too low to attend, and she would understand without needing to pry any further. She in turn gave my parents her home telephone number and asked them to keep her up to date with what was happening. She had seen me working with children and had noted my passion for working with children with special needs. And that helped hugely – probably more than she realised actually – as by now my confidence had reached rock bottom. Having somebody offer much needed support was in itself very comforting, but having spent time with me and observed me working with children, her offer was much more significant and meant the world to me at the time, as her confidence in my abilities did not falter once.

The fact that I had already told the university about what was happening was irrelevant as far as this second meeting was concerned, though, as there would undoubtedly have been repercussions had the university been officially notified that I was suspected of child sexual abuse. Perhaps at that point the university would have been left with no other option than to ask me to leave.

My solicitor was notified of the decision late that afternoon and he in turn contacted my parents. We had just eaten our tea in silence, all of us feeling pretty anxious. The decision had been made – the meeting had decided that the university should be notified.

My life was over. At least that was how I felt, and probably how my parents felt too. Perhaps this was as hard for them, if not harder, having to watch me trying to comprehend what was happening, and knowing what it meant for my future. All I had wanted to do since getting to know Sarah was train to be a teacher and spend my life working with children with special needs; I found it extremely rewarding and very enjoyable. The thought of working in a job that could offer me this was very exciting, especially as I hadn't really known what I wanted to do up until this point. But now it looked as if this part of my life was finished too.

And I did feel upset with our GP following the meeting, as I thought one of the two families might, not because he had taken sides, but because it appeared from the outside that he must have been prepared to believe that I had abused Sarah and was therefore satisfied that the university should be notified. Without having detailed minutes, I could never be certain how involved he was with the decision about informing the university. But for me his mere attendance at the meeting would itself have repercussions.

From that point on I avoided ever going to our surgery unless absolutely necessary, and those occasions were rare. I was utterly convinced that none of the doctors there would see me willingly, if they had had a choice, and that everybody at the surgery would treat me with contempt. I just could not face the risk of any more upset, so I stayed away. But there were many, many times, especially in the early days following this terrible trauma, when I was in desperate need of some medical help or professional support, but was too scared to ever ask.

I cried and cried and cried. Where did we go from here?

All I can say is, thank goodness for determined parents! Numerous telephone calls took place that evening and late into the night. The telephone was still ringing at 11.30pm – a friend of my parents who, thank goodness, was able to offer some practical help. Emotional support is great too, and was much needed by all of us, but what we really needed right now was concrete advice and hands-on help.

At 4pm the following day Mr Smith, the social worker, arrived at our house for a meeting that had been arranged through my parents the previous evening. I know the meeting lasted around two and a half hours, but unfortunately the majority of what was discussed remains a complete blur to me. I remember him arriving and leaving but, other than one very vivid conversation that will remain with me for ever, very little of what happened in between.

I know now that this lack of memory was my coping mechanism; I just could not take any more. My parents were at this meeting too, and they were absolutely furious that the decision to notify my university had been made without allowing me any representation other than a written report. According to my mum's notes of the meeting, my parents stated their belief that Sally and Jim had, through their actions, led the social services (and police) to think that I may have harmed Sarah, and now they were telling anybody willing to listen the same thing.

My parents told Mr Smith that they would take whatever course of action was necessary to stop the university being notified, and if this meant going to court, so be it.

Before this meeting, mum and I had spent the day talking

about what was going to happen, and I had asked her what would happen if I ever decided to have children of my own. I was now starting to worry that this part of my life, too, might be cruelly taken away, just as everything else seemed to have been. Mum told me not to worry, but I could see the anxiety etched on her face too. She knew that I'd wanted from a very young age to have children, and even today tells the story of me saying that I wanted to have five sons one day! I must have been around seventeen or eighteen years old when my maternal instincts kicked in, and I'm sure had I met Mr Right then that I would probably have had children very soon after.

As I said, I recall very little other than one particular conversation at the meeting with Mr Smith. Mum repeated the question to him that I had asked her earlier in the day about having children of my own one day, and Mr Smith's response was that there would in fact be no guarantees I would not have my own children taken away from me. My mum, disbelieving, I think, asked him to repeat his answer, and the three of us sat in absolute horror listening once more to his reply, trying hard to take on board what he was saying.

There was no certainty, if I ever had children, that I would be allowed to keep them.

At this point I left the room, and found myself sitting at the bottom of the stairs, head in hands, numb with sadness and disbelief. As if everything that had happened to date wasn't bad enough. What did the future have in store for me now; what was there to look forward to? My career seemed to be over before it had even begun, and now my dream of becoming a mother one day also seemed to be in jeopardy. I was in such a state of shock. I didn't know which way to turn, whether there was anything or anybody out there who could stop this rollercoaster of a nightmare. Right now I felt as if the bottom had dropped out of my world.

There really was no way in which this situation could be any worse. Why had Sally and Jim been so determined for this to happen, to inflict such cruelty on somebody they had always previously had complete trust in and respect for? And why, oh why, couldn't these police officers, these social workers, read between the lines and question exactly the same things I was questioning? Why were they allowing themselves to be so seemingly led by Sally and Jim? While I do not know a great deal about their professional training, I would like to think that one fundamental piece of training would be for anyone conducting such investigations to consider all possibilities, to be objective, not to be misled by any of the parties involved. Yet from the start the police and then the social services seemed to be completely taken in by Sally and Jim. Could this be due to the fact that Sarah had special needs and therefore had a greater degree of vulnerability? Perhaps they had become more emotionally involved with the family than they might with other cases because of this. Whatever the reason, it was wrong, and the outcome for both Sarah and me was wrong too.

I cannot remember much about the rest of the meeting at all. I know that my mum went on to discuss the fact that Sarah, as well as Thomas and Milly, were not the only children I ever came into contact with. Therefore, if the social services were planning to notify the university about their concerns, perhaps they should widen this and notify the parents of every child I had ever looked after, whether through babysitting or at the local group I had taken Sarah to, and even my aunt, whose daughter I spent time with. I was very close to one cousin in particular, partly because I was also her godmother; she and I spent time together and I took her out for the day occasionally. Were the social services going to notify her mum, too? Mr Smith agreed that there would be no point in notifying the university unless they also notified every place where I was likely to come in to contact with children.

During the meeting he also added that he would not be confident enough in me to allow me to look after his own children. How appropriate it was for him to make such a personal comment I am unsure, but it was very hurtful, and could only have been intended to cause upset. This was the first time I had heard anybody say they would not feel confident in allowing me to be around their children, and this has had a terrible impact on me over a very long period of time.

My dad told Mr Smith that if he thought for one minute I might have harmed Sarah, or any other child for that matter, he would have got me help; he certainly would not have ignored it just because I was his daughter. I felt that this comment, as well as all the other things we were saying, fell on deaf ears though; whatever any of us said we seemed to be in a no-win situation – decisions were being made, I felt, without our thoughts or feelings being taken into consideration.

Much further down the line, I obtained the notes Mr Smith made following this meeting; interestingly, he did not record what he told us about my future as far as having children was concerned. The notes do state that he, "Could not rule out the possibility that Sarah (a) had not been abused, and (b) if she had, had been abused by somebody completely different." Yet it felt to me as if both of these significant points were being completely ignored, even now. I really could not understand why he was writing these thoughts down, yet he was still prepared to notify the university. There seemed to be a complete disregard for me and the effect that their decision might well have on my life and future career, even though he seemed to be admitting his own doubts. His notes say that he did agree to pass all of my parents' comments and concerns to his manager prior to taking any action in terms of notifying the university, and thankfully he did keep to his word on this, but I doubted even that would make any difference to anything.

The next morning my parents telephoned Philip Dawes, who had by this time enlisted the assistance of a second solicitor who had greater experience of the social services. His name was James Millichap. A meeting with both was arranged for the following week, the purpose of which would be to serve an injunction on the social services and prevent them from contacting my university, if they were determined to continue with this course of action.

In between the meeting with Mr Smith and the meeting due to take place with my solicitors, my parents managed to arrange a meeting at the local social services offices with the District Children and Families Manager (Mr Smith's manager) and the County Assistant Director of Social Services. The purpose as far as my parents and I were concerned was to get the decision to notify the university overturned.

I remember that both individuals listened attentively to what we said, but they admitted that they did not have all of the facts of the case to hand and were therefore not able to respond to every issue we raised. We were given every opportunity to talk about the situation as we saw it, to voice our concerns about the possible misinterpretation of Sarah's signing in her interview, to say that we believed Sarah appeared to have been primed, and to tell them that we believed Sally and Jim had appeared to point the finger at me from very early on in the investigation.

By the time of this meeting I had started to do some research of my own, and reading various pieces of research relating to child sexual abuse, it became clear to me that the majority of this type of abuse is carried out by a male who is known to the child, often the father or stepfather. Research statistics vary from study to study, but in one example the findings show that women are the perpetrators in just 1–4% of cases. If you then remove the number of women alleged to abuse boys, the percentage allegedly abusing girls is even lower. I had brought some of these statistics to the meeting, but in actual fact these two individuals were already fully aware of the statistics, as I suppose they would have to be. The County Assistant Director even admitted that he had never before, in his experience of more than one thousand abuse cases, come across a female abusing a female.

It was at this point that my dad stood up and said he could see no point in continuing with the meeting. Why on earth should his daughter fall into this tiny percentage of people, when research showed that in at least 96% of cases the perpetrator was male?

It was agreed that the facts of this case would be looked at again in detail, both by the County Assistant Director and by his legal department, prior to any action being taken to inform the university.

Regardless of the outcome, I would always be grateful for this meeting and for being listened to. I had said all along that in some ways I wished I had been charged, as I would at least have had the opportunity to stand up in court and put my points across. It had felt all along as though I wasn't being given the chance to say what I thought – that everybody had already made their minds up and therefore anything I said was deemed irrelevant. It was a relief to be able finally to voice everything that we all felt needed to be said. And perhaps in a way it was a blessing that it had taken so long for this moment to happen, as up until fairly recently I had refused to even accept the possibility that Sarah might have been abused or that Sally and Jim might be trying to influence the outcome of the investigation.

Philip Dawes received a letter from the District Children and Families Manager three days later, confirming that the case would be reviewed and that there would be no contact with the university until the review had been concluded.

I couldn't get my hopes up, not yet; nothing so far had gone my way and I did not believe that anything would change now. They offered to read everything that had been said and consider everything that had happened, and presumably this would include the paediatrician's findings, the police interviews and all social worker notes too. But unless they were really prepared to take on board everything that we had said to them at our meeting, I felt convinced that they were bound to reach the same conclusions.

In the meantime, we met with both Philip Dawes and James Millichap, and they sent a letter to the social services reiterating all of the reasons we had brought up at the meeting, as well as more of their own, to press for the university not to be notified of their concerns. The reasons listed included the two meetings that had previously taken place and the unfairness of both. Sally and Jim had been directly involved with the first, but had had representation at both. I had had no representation at either, and therefore no opportunities to confront or challenge anything that was said.

James Millichap received a telephone call just a few days later from the District Children and Families Manager, confirming that as a result of the review, the decision to notify the university had been overturned. Plus, no other body where I had come into contact with children would be told.

To say that I jumped for joy would be inaccurate and inappropriate, as I was still completely and utterly devastated by everything that had happened. However, the decision was a massive relief, and would at least mean that I could continue with my studies and hopefully get on with my life once more.

Six

But where would I go from here? Did I want to carry on with my studies and train to be a special needs teacher, after everything that had happened? My confidence, not only in myself, but in my ability to work with children, was shattered. Could it ever be repaired?

For quite some months after this horrific period in my life I struggled to function at all, and for some years afterwards I continued to suffer from severe anxiety. I decided that in the short term I needed some time out, and it was agreed with my tutor and the university that I should take the rest of the term off, as a kind of sick leave. This was an important term as far as the course was concerned, involving a lengthy teaching practice, and I knew I was not in any fit state to take this on right now. My tutor was once again fantastically supportive.

During these tough months, I seem to have unconsciously used a blanking or coping mechanism; I have very little recollection of what I did during my time off from university. I was extremely depressed and spent quite a bit of time in bed. It was so hard trying to come to terms with what had happened, especially as the situation with Sarah was, in my eyes, not yet resolved. I had no idea whether or not she had been abused; all I knew was that if she had been, the abuse could very easily still be going on. As far as I could tell, I was the only suspect the police and social services had and so presumably the investigation would now be closed, as their enquiries had been exhausted. This worried me greatly, but I knew there was absolutely nothing I could do about it.

Life living in the same village as Sarah and her family was tough going, too. Sally and Jim took full advantage of the fact that they ran a busy shop there, telling their customers that I was suspected of abusing their daughter. I knew many of these people by now too, as they had been 'my' customers; but sadly many of them no longer wanted to talk to me. Some even went as far as crossing to the other side of the road so that they would not have to pass me on the pavement. I could not believe that they would treat me with such animosity unless what they had been told was not strictly accurate, but of course there was no way of knowing what they were being told.

I have read many media articles during recent years calling for anonymity for the accused in cases like mine. Having now experienced people's reactions first hand, I would certainly agree that we should be entitled to anonymity, at least until the point of being charged. The accuser is granted anonymity, and it would surely only be fair if the accused is too. One of the fundamental arguments against anonymity for the accused in some of the more high profile cases of recent years has been the desire on the part of the police to encourage more alleged victims to come forward and report what happened to them.

Sadly I believe that this can only increase the number of false allegations from individuals who see an opportunity to claim compensation or just to wreck the life of a personality who has achieved much. Many of these cases have been historical, with the alleged abuse taking place sometimes decades previously. I feel that there ought to be a maximum period of time placed on these allegations being reported; how can anyone defend themselves against an allegation from twenty or thirty years ago.

I'm sure that my life might not have become quite so distressing if Sally and Jim had been prevented from disclosing my name to anybody; I felt as if my good character was being completely destroyed. Why would they want to talk to people about what had happened anyway? Perhaps they felt they needed support, not just from their immediate family but from anyone prepared to offer it. I was quite the opposite, I suppose, quite a private person as far as my personal business was concerned, and therefore reluctant to talk to just anyone.

As hard as I tried, it was virtually impossible to carry on living anything like a normal life. My parents' advice always was to hold my head high, to look people in the eye and smile, but it was so hard. I was still only twenty years old, and trying to find my way in the world; I just had no idea how to deal with the life I was now faced with. There were numerous occasions when I arrived home in tears, having been given the silent treatment, or a particularly vicious glare or worse still a cruel comment, by somebody who just a few months ago would have stopped for a chat. I didn't have the ability to deal with this sort of treatment; it was alien to me.

I remember one individual speaking to me in the local

pub, but only to tell me that the reason I wasn't charged was because Sarah had special needs and would therefore have been an unreliable witness. This was so hurtful. Did these people really believe what they were being told? The real reason I wasn't charged was that there was virtually no evidence suggesting that Sarah had even been abused, let alone by me. Perhaps her disabilities might have had an impact on her reliability as a witness, I don't know, but there is no doubt in my mind that I would certainly have been charged if there had been enough evidence.

But the facts of the case weren't important to these people. They thrived on village gossip; I had witnessed that myself numerous times in the past while working in the shop. The more scandalous the story, the more they loved it, regardless of the truth.

Not only was I sent to Coventry by the majority of those to whom Sally or Jim told their version of what had happened, I was also told that I was no longer needed as a helper at the group I had been taking Sarah to. This didn't really come as any surprise, the lady running the group would either have received the information first hand from Sally or heard the rumours that were circulating. I assumed that somebody else would take over. Either that or Sarah would not go to the group any more, which would be a pity for her. Being told that I was no longer needed was very hard to accept though; I was in a pretty vulnerable state by now. Life had previously been so good, but now I just couldn't see anything positive anywhere. I had absolutely no enthusiasm for anything anymore.

All I really wanted to do was shout from the rooftops that I was still the same person these people had known for the last four or five years, some for much longer than that.

I hadn't changed, and I hadn't done anything wrong. But unlike Sally and Jim, I didn't have an outlet like the shop to talk to people. Nobody ever approached me to enquire about what happened; they just seemed content to believe what Sally or Jim had told them, or what they heard from others. But perhaps I would have reacted the same way in their situation. Was I expecting too much of people to find the courage to ask me directly; they might feel too embarrassed. Quite possibly I suppose, but it didn't make the situation any easier to deal with. I had no self-confidence left, and even though my solicitor had suggested fighting fire with fire, I felt so totally worthless that by now I was starting to believe that my place really was in the gutter. I knew that I was innocent, but that made no difference to the way I felt, and I had no confidence to be able to start talking openly about what had happened. Apart from anything else, speaking out would mean being disloyal to Sally and Jim, and despite everything, that was still something I struggled with and felt guilty about. They had been a huge part of my life for a number of years; I had felt comfortable around them and we had had much fun together. That period of my life wasn't something that could be easily forgotten and while I struggled to understand why they had treated me the way they had, I still felt very attached to them and missed them greatly. They had depended on me for help, but I had also started to depend on them for friendship, and I could not speak unkindly about them, even to those closest to me.

I did not spend my time away from university very well, that much I do know. I am certain that my parents felt helpless, not knowing what they could do to help put things right. They are very practical people and would have felt frustrated that there was nothing obvious they could do.

I knew I needed time away from university, but I had no real plans. Days were endless. I would go for long drives in my car, listen to music, reflect on what had happened during these dreadful months. But I could not move forward at all, as this would mean leaving some very happy times behind, and I somehow convinced myself that even now things might go back to the way they were before the abuse investigation had begun.

During this time away from university I turned twenty one. I had always planned to celebrate in style, to have a big party, but this was the last thing I felt like doing, particularly as there would be some very special people missing from the guest list. But my parents took it upon themselves to organise a small party behind my back, determined that we should try to do something normal and to celebrate my big day. They wanted to mark this milestone. They hired a small hall locally and organised a caterer and a disco. My university friends all travelled down, Martha came along, some family members, and my parents too of course. Laura was still abroad, unfortunately, but it was a really lovely evening. I managed to relax and have some fun with my friends, and I had quite a bit to drink but that was acceptable under the circumstances! My parents had definitely made the right decision. I did feel very sad, but surrounded by the love and support I had made the evening one to remember, and my photograph album from this occasion is stacked full of lovely memories.

Unfortunately though, by the time I needed to think about going back to my studies I was no further forward than I had been. I was still utterly depressed and lacking in motivation. To this day I have no idea how, but somehow I managed to claw back enough drive to carry on with my second year of university and I successfully completed a teaching project that had to be carried out before the end of the summer term.

Once back studying again, I approached the local primary school in our village and asked for a group of children to participate in this teaching project. I think I had chosen to look at phonics teaching. The headteacher had willingly agreed and I was allocated certain times each week over a period of a few weeks when I would go in to the school. By now both Thomas and Milly were pupils at this school, but I had no intention of working with either of them; it would have been completely inappropriate but anyway they were not in the right age group. I was trying to hold my head high and carry on my life as normally as possible but the decision to go in to this school and so soon after the abuse investigation, turned out to be a mistake, as I would soon learn.

It had taken a huge amount of courage to do this project, as my confidence with children had been destroyed completely. I had no faith in myself and my abilities any more, and actually found myself feeling quite panicky around children. Perhaps subconsciously I was now feeling threatened by them – or more likely by their parents – and by what could potentially happen. My experiences with Sally and Jim had left a permanent scar, and I now felt unable to trust a soul. It was a horrible feeling, leaving me isolated and very lonely. I think that apart from my parents and my friends Laura and Martha, I felt uneasy about everybody, and assumed that everyone was talking about me and what I had supposedly done. Paranoia is an awful condition to suffer from, and to a degree I still suffer today, although thankfully to a much lesser extent.

I must first of all talk more about Laura. By the time

of my arrest she and I had a great friendship, having spent much time together over the four years we had known each other. In many ways we were very similar, with similar hopes and dreams for our futures; we both dreamed of getting married and having children one day, and of having successful careers. We seemed to think in similar ways, and this is, I'm sure, what kept the friendship strong. We always seemed to know what the other was thinking. It was actually a very warm feeling, knowing that I had somebody like that in my life.

Unfortunately, when I was arrested Laura was spending a year abroad as part of her degree course. We were still in contact by letter, and I remember only too well sitting down on my bed and trying to write her a letter explaining what was happening. I had been in two minds about telling her, but knew she would be upset to find out at a later date. It was a hard letter to write, not only because I knew that Laura would be upset to read it, but because seeing it written down made the situation even more real.

As soon as Laura received the letter, she had been on the telephone to me. It must have cost her an absolute fortune to call, but I was so pleased to hear from her and to know that I at least had her support. I think she even offered to come home so that she was close by, but I told her that really wasn't necessary. How kind though. It meant so much. We kept in even closer contact throughout the rest of the time she was abroad. I needed her support so very much, and even from such a distance she was an amazing friend.

Laura never once doubted me or questioned my guilt, not because we were friends but because she believed in me. There have been more times than I care to remember when I have needed huge amounts of emotional support but she has always been there to help. We have been through so much together, good and bad times, but our friendship has always been strong enough to deal with anything that life throws at us. I'm not sure whether I would be in such a good place now had I not had Laura in my life, and for that I am eternally thankful. Laura is married these days and has a beautiful little girl – my goddaughter.

So, I had a placement in the local primary school to carry out my teaching project. I went to the school on the days and times allocated and worked with a group of around six children. I was given a small space in the school hall to work with them, and to start with everything was fine.

About two thirds of the way through my project, I arrived home from university one day to find a handwritten letter on the doorstep from the headteacher. He had withdrawn his permission for me to carry out the study at his school. We later discovered that Sally had found out I was doing my project and she had threatened to remove Thomas and Milly from the school if I was allowed to continue. She had also contacted the police to tell them I was working at the school. I have no idea what she expected them to do about it. I guess the headteacher didn't want to cause any upset, so the easiest option for him had been to ask me to leave. At the time it was pretty humiliating and very upsetting, but looking back I do understand the difficult position that I must have put him in. I would probably have reacted the same way if I was him.

It was around this time that my parents had decided to request the assistance of the police to help deal with a number of problems we had encountered following the abuse investigation. I was feeling completely overwhelmed with what felt like relentless unkindness from some locals, and we were all feeling uncertain about how best to deal with things. My parents got in touch with a more senior person, the superintendent for our area. I must say that I was not overjoyed once I learned of their decision to involve the police in our lives, but they seemed to feel that it was necessary.

Ever since the possibility that Sarah had been abused had become public knowledge, thanks in part to Sally and Jim and the inevitable gossiping that followed, my life in the village (and probably my parents' lives, too) had become more and more difficult. As I have already said, there were so many occasions when I experienced nasty comments from people in the street, and at times both Sally and Jim swore at me or assaulted me physically. I remember Sally pushing me off a pavement and knocking into me. One other incident has stuck in my mind more than most, and still gives me nightmares today. A lady who lived locally, and who must presumably have listened to and believed the gossip about me, attempted to push me down a flight of marble stairs in a shop in our local town. Had I lost my footing, I would certainly have been badly injured, if not worse. Life was unbearable and I had reached the point where I was too scared to leave the house on my own.

The incident at the school was probably my own silly fault, but these other incidents seemed to be the result of Sally and Jim's anger or frustration that I had not been punished. They were determined to make my life a misery, and they did a good job. Surely by now, I thought, even they had to admit that I might not have done anything wrong? Why were they carrying on this way? Perhaps they wanted to make sure the locals kept on believing that I was the guilty party. I felt that they were very unhappy seeing me around the village, on the odd occasions I did venture out, and perhaps they felt their approach might make me leave for good, especially if enough people turned on me. I couldn't begin to understand what was going on in their lives or in their heads that would make them behave this way towards me, it was incredibly harsh, and at times almost impossible not to react.

As well as lots of these minor incidents, Sally also reported me to the police for dangerous driving. I suppose it shouldn't have come as any surprise that she would stoop so very low, but nevertheless when the police got in touch and asked to make an appointment to discuss the incident, I was once more terrified about what might happen. My trust in both the police and the social services had been destroyed completely as a result of what I saw as their incompetence throughout the abuse investigation, and the last thing I wanted now was to have to deal with any of them again. The dangerous driving to which they were referring had not been dangerous driving at all, and thankfully I had had Martha in the car with me on the occasion they were referring to, and she was also able to provide a statement for the police.

I had arrived at a road junction in to our village at exactly the same time as Sally, from opposite directions. The road we were both turning in to had a "Road Closed" sign at the junction. I knew that the road was accessible, but Sally had stopped and seemed uncertain about proceeding. So rather than sit and wait for her to decide what to do, I had taken the decision to cross the road and enter the village, driving in front of Sally's car. Sadly, Sally's version of this was somewhat different to mine, the inference being that I had intended to drive into her, or at least to scare her. This could not have been further from the truth.

Needless to say, nothing came of this incident and I was

not charged, but once again, firstly through her actions about the school project and now by reporting me for dangerous driving, Sally seemed intent on making my life miserable.

So, my parents asked the superintendent for his help in the matter, and in fairness to him, he did try to assist. I know that he visited the headteacher at the local primary school, and although I was never reinstated, I believe he was at least able to point out the facts of the case as we knew them, and we felt that this was a positive move.

He also agreed to have a look at the case again. In particular, he said he planned to approach the paediatrician with a view to trying to ascertain the likelihood that abuse had definitely taken place. This resulted from the first meeting we had with him, during which we voiced our concerns about the way the investigation had been carried out, along with the repercussions for me now trying to rebuild my life living in the same village as Sally and Jim. On the face of it, he seemed genuinely concerned, and was certainly prepared to spend some time taking a look back at everything that had happened. He even offered to send Sally and Jim a copy of the letter the police had received from the CPS, which stated categorically that there was no clear evidence Sarah had even been abused, which we felt would be a good idea.

Unfortunately, though, nothing else positive ever came from his involvement. I do believe that he looked back through the paperwork, and he did go and talk to Sally and Jim. My parents and I were then invited back to the police station for a follow-up meeting with the superintendent. He told us that, having read through all of the material, he could see no reason to reopen the investigation; there was no fresh evidence and there did not seem to be any point in going over ground already covered. I was disappointed that he felt this way, but all of these investigations do take time, and as there were no new avenues to explore, I guess his decision was fair. I was surprised to hear that Sally and Jim had apparently told him it was their intention to get us to move out of the village. Their behaviour certainly indicated that this was true, but hearing it from him was a shock.

He went on to tell us something so upsetting that I felt physically sick. Sally and Jim had told him that Sarah was not expected to live a great deal longer. For this reason they requested to be left alone to spend what time they had left with their daughter. The superintendent felt that this was also a good enough reason not to reopen the investigation, and at the time I would have agreed, in spite of my disappointment. I would not have wanted Sarah to endure anything else in the way of examinations or interviews, and although my feelings towards Sally and Jim were now tainted, I would also have agreed that they should be allowed that special time with Sarah.

My parents and I left the meeting that day with great sadness in our hearts. I wished more than anything in the world that I might be allowed to see Sarah just one more time, to give her a final cuddle and tell her that she would always have a special place in my heart. But sadly that would never be.

I had to cope with this new information and at the same time accept that we had done all we could in trying to get to the bottom of what really had or had not happened to Sarah. The police were not going to reopen the investigation, so I had to face the reality that people would probably continue to point the finger at me for some time to come, at least until another juicy piece of gossip shook the streets of our village.

Miraculously, though, I did see Sarah one more time, a year or so after the investigation had been closed. I had walked down to the village to post a letter, and out of the corner of my eye as I approached the postbox I saw a group of youngsters walking in my direction. I was still very damaged at this point, and more often than not walked with my head down and not making eye contact with anyone; I somehow thought I would not be noticed if I didn't look at people. For some reason, though, I looked up at this moment, and among the group of children I spotted Sarah. My heart started beating rapidly – I desperately wanted to see her but knew I should not approach her or the group she was with. However, Sarah had already spotted me and she was sobbing. What should I do? She was trotting towards me; the adult helper in the group was Martha and she was trying unsuccessfully to hold on to her. Sarah reached me and threw her arms round me. She clung to me and all I could do was what came naturally to me; I gave her the biggest cuddle ever. I too wanted to cry, but I needed to maintain my composure, at least until I got home. Sarah looked up at me and made the signs for "home" and "friend". I think she was saying that she wanted to come to my house, something she and her siblings had often done in previous years, but I could not be sure. She could just as easily be signing that she wanted me to go to her house. I told her that she could not come to my house, but whether or not she understood I do not know. She would at least have understood that I was saying no. I also told her that I loved her very much; this was a sign I knew she was familiar with. I then gave her another cuddle and had to walk away. I think she would probably have held on to me for much longer, but in fairness to Martha I had to walk away.

I spoke to Martha later that same day, and she told me that she had later struggled to get Sarah past our house; she had been absolutely determined to come and see me.

I had had that last time with Sarah, and I will always remember, with great fondness but much sadness, our final cuddle. What a special girl.

Seeing Sarah again somehow gave me renewed inner strength, and I managed to plod on with my studies. In a way I felt I owed it to her to try to complete my degree course, as it was she who had inspired me in the first place. I completed my second year successfully; thankfully I had been able to collect adequate information from the project I had undertaken in the primary school and actually gained quite a high mark for my work.

At the end of the second year, three of my university friends started talking about renting a student house on campus for the third, so that they would have more regular access to the libraries and generally be able to spend more time on their work. The third year was apparently quite a tough one, and we were all spending a fair amount of time travelling to and from university at both ends of the day. Renting a house seemed a great idea, and now that I didn't have Sally and the children to go back to each evening, I decided I was interested in joining the girls in looking for a house.

We found a lovely three-bedroomed house about two miles from our college. It was already a student house and was owned by an elderly lady who lived just a few doors away. The area was reasonable, which was important as we were all young girls moving away from home for the first time.

So, in September the four of us moved in together. It was

quite an exciting time, although I was still struggling hugely to cope with life in general. I suffered from extreme paranoia, and my confidence was at rock bottom. But perhaps this year away from home might be just what the doctor ordered? My friends were incredibly supportive and although they could never really put themselves in my position, they always tried to say and do the right things, and that meant so much to me. But I think I made them laugh quite a bit too; they were all city girls but I was the typical country bumpkin. I don't think I had even ever locked my car up at night when I was living at home with my parents; my friends couldn't believe that there was anywhere in the world where this wasn't necessary, and I needed constant reminders about it when I went back to our pad at the end of each day.

The first term of our third year was even more important to me, as I had to face a lengthy teaching practice just a few weeks into the term. This should have been carried out during my second year, but as I had taken a lot of time off I had had to miss it. The other girls had already successfully completed theirs. My tutor knew how utterly petrified I was about going into a school and being around children again, and she kindly found me a placement at a school not too far from my parents' house, so that I could go home to them each evening. This would mean being away from my friends and our new home for a few weeks, but it felt like the best way. She really was trying to make things as easy for me as she could; we were usually expected to carry out placements near the university, as we would be visited regularly by tutors to see how we were getting on and to assess our progress. My being placed almost sixty miles from the university meant that somebody was going to have to make long trips to come and visit me.

I surprised myself by thoroughly enjoying the time I spent at the school. The staff were lovely and the children even more so. My time there reminded me of how much I had wanted to be a teacher and, to a degree, restored my confidence in myself. The tutor assigned to assess my progress was new to me; I knew who she was but we had never met before. Whether or not she knew what had happened to me I do not know, but she visited the school two or three times in total and wrote a glowing final report, saying that she felt I had a natural way with children, and that I would make a brilliant teacher in the future.

I remember her sitting in on one maths lesson I had prepared. It was a little risky, as it would involve the children getting out of their seats and coming up to the front of the class to participate. These sorts of activities were always a little uncertain, as children were unpredictable at the best of times and you needed to feel confident about being able to deal with whatever they threw at you. But the risk had been well worth it – the children had behaved remarkably well, responded well to the lesson, and the tutor rewarded me with this excellent report.

Sadly though, even by this point I think I knew there was little likelihood that I would ever teach, if indeed I could find the strength to even complete the course. I knew how much I loved being around children, and they did seem to respond well to me in the classroom environment. My problem was an absolute fear that the same situation that had arisen with Sarah and her family might arise again. I had known and cared about these people, yet look at what they had allowed to happen to me. They wouldn't have cared if I had been charged or even convicted of a crime I had not committed. If they were prepared to allow this to happen, surely anybody else would be the same. If I were a teacher with a class of thirty children, that meant thirty children who may potentially have been abused by somebody and, even more importantly, thirty families who could point the finger of blame at me. I knew there was no way I could put myself in that position. I needed to protect myself from anything like that ever happening again.

You might argue that I need not have bothered to complete the degree course if I had no intention of ever teaching. And I would agree with this argument, except that I felt an inner desire to prove to those people, who now doubted me, that I could do it, and that nothing was going to stop me achieving what I had set out to achieve. I also needed to try to restore my confidence, and this was perhaps one way of doing just that.

We had a great third year at university. I had moved back into the student house a few weeks later, having successfully completed my teaching practice. By this time the other three girls had all settled in, but they made every effort when I got back, and we had such fun. We weren't party animals, but preferred to stay in during the evenings watching television or doing some university project or other. Three of us were taking the same course, and we could help each other and work together on some projects. We did go out a few times, and had a few friends over in the evenings. We all went home at the weekends, though. This was my first time living away from home, and it was nice to go back at the weekends for a catch-up with my parents and getting my washing done was an added bonus!

There were still times during my final two years at university when I found myself doubting my abilities, and there were many occasions when I sat with my tutor explaining that I wasn't sure I could continue with the course. However, between her and my lovely group of friends, who all made many, many allowances for me during those years of studying, somehow I made it, and after four gruelling years we all graduated. We felt such a sense of achievement, but none more than me. It felt sad that Sarah would not be part of my celebrations, as she had inspired me in the first place, but I hoped she would always have the same fond memories that I had of our times together.

It was hard to believe that I had actually made it, but graduation day arrived and it was an amazing feeling to be standing alongside my friends celebrating our success. For my parents too this was a special day, as they had been through these tough times with me. Their pride was obvious for all to see. The other girls had all been busy applying for teaching posts during our final term, and every one of them had a new job lined up that autumn to prepare for. I was so pleased for them all; they would be fantastic teachers.

But my final term had had its ups and downs. I had completed my teaching practices and everybody told me what a great teacher I could be. My decision not to apply for teaching posts started to falter. Perhaps I could do it; perhaps I could erase the awful memories of what had happened and start afresh. I saw an advert in a local paper for a teacher in one of the many primary schools in our area and decided, impulsively, to apply for it.

It didn't cross my mind for one minute that anything would come from the application. I was sure the school would receive hundreds of applications, and not all schools would want somebody straight out of university. But this school was interested and I was invited for an interview. To say that I was scared would be an understatement. This was not going to be the usual kind of interview either – the school was looking for somebody who could play the piano in school assemblies and on other occasions. I was going to have to play a solo piece. Yikes! I had actually reached grade five on the piano, but that was several years earlier, and I was extremely rusty and certainly lacked the confidence needed to play in front of an audience.

At the interview I somehow fumbled my way through a well-known hymn, but it was awful. My hands were shaking uncontrollably, which didn't help. I was also interviewed by a panel that consisted of the headteacher and several governors. This was just as scary as playing the hymn; my mouth felt dry and I was convinced that they could all tell just from looking at me that I had been accused of abusing a child. I continued to suffer from paranoia, such a debilitating condition. I left the school that day with no doubt in my mind that I would not be successful. However, within an hour or two of arriving home, I received a telephone call from the headteacher offering me the job.

Wow. How on earth had I managed that? I was, in some ways, very proud of myself. I could do it if I tried. I was just the same as all of my friends; we would all start work together later that year after all, as had been the intention right back at the start of our studies four years earlier. That evening my parents and I went out for a meal to celebrate. Perhaps life would work out OK after all.

But overnight my old fears reappeared. I had a sleepless night; everything was going round in my head. Everything that had happened with Sally and Jim, and everything that could happen again if I was faced with a classroom full of children. I was panicking uncontrollably. I think I had known all along, in my heart of hearts, that I would not be able to hold down a teaching job. But I had wanted to fit in with my friends and so had determined to do the same as they were doing. But they didn't have any of the hang-ups I had. I didn't resent them for that, I just felt sad that my life was different.

So after a sleepless night I made the decision to contact the school and turn down the position I had been offered. I knew they would think this strange, but I couldn't begin to explain things to them. I wrote a letter to the headteacher and although I cannot remember what reason I gave for turning the job down, I know that I did not tell her the truth. My decision had been made; I needed to start to think about other careers I might pursue, or perhaps look at starting a new course, studying something completely different.

Sadly, that summer we had more heartache to deal with. My brother, now aged 25, died suddenly and unexpectedly. I haven't talked about him a great deal in the book, for no other reason than the fact that he had long flown the nest when my troubles started and so he doesn't feature greatly during this period in my life. My parents and I had made the conscious decision that he did not need to know what was happening, he did not need any upset in his life, and so he had remained blissfully unaware of what was happening back at home. He had left home at 18, been to university and was now setting up home with his long-term girlfriend. He was absolutely hopeless at keeping in touch with any of us, which my parents constantly moaned about, but that made it even easier to protect him from the devastation we were all suffering. He was a very sensitive person, quiet and thoughtful, and we believed that he would not have coped at all with knowing what I was going through, hence our decision not to tell him.

Having to deal with his death was terribly hard, but we all supported each other once more and somehow found a way of carrying on. It has taken years, and although life will never be the same, we have found the strength to get on with our lives. I think about him often.

Some months later, I came across a university advertisement for students to apply for a Master's degree. The advert was quite appealing, and I started to seriously consider the idea of more studying. This would mean further financial support from my parents, but I hoped they would be happy to provide this. They were worried, I know, that I was now faced with an uncertain future and a particularly difficult period in which all of my university friends would be starting their teaching posts, and they wanted me to keep as busy as possible. I continued to suffer emotionally over what had happened. Anxiety was a real issue, and I struggled with depression too, although I didn't admit it to anyone until many years later.

I was right; my parents were just happy that I wasn't going to lie in bed all day. They thought that more studying was the perfect solution. I started to look at the types of courses I might study and straight away I found a research-based course. This was completely different to some Master's courses, which were more or less identical in style to the degree I had already done, with lectures on your chosen subject and then exams at the end of the course. The course I had found would instead involve carrying out research into a chosen area of interest and then writing a dissertation at the end. This sounded much more exciting, and I already had an idea of the area of research I would like to study.

It was now three years since the police and social services had been involved in our lives, and it was time to try to move on. Without any hesitation I applied to study for the degree. I had chosen a different university, thinking that there were still too many sad memories at the place I had carried out my teacher training. I was invited for interview and readily accepted on to the course. I think that the time frame for completing my studies was reasonably flexible, but I planned to carry out the research over a period of around twelve months, and then write the dissertation during the second year.

An initial meeting was arranged with the man who would be my tutor. He would support me and offer help along the way, both with my research and the dissertation, but it turned out that he wasn't particularly enthusiastic about the subject I planned to research.

I had decided that it would be interesting to research false allegations of sexual abuse; false allegations were a fairly new phenomenon that had been highlighted in the press by large cases such as Orkney and Cleveland, but into which not many people in the UK had yet carried out any research. Most of the research that did exist at that time was American.

I also wondered whether I might find it therapeutic in some way, and whether I might meet others who had had similar experiences to me. But I knew that, if I was going to carry out a worthwhile piece of research, it had to be completely unbiased, and I would need to get opinions from professionals working in that area too. Ironically, it turned out that my tutor had previously been a social worker, and for that reason I think he struggled to accept the research I wanted to carry out. However, he didn't have any choice; the university had accepted what I wanted to do and his role now was to help and guide me through the process.

And so I spent the next two years working on my research project. I struggled to persuade many professionals to participate, but in the end did achieve interviews with a small number of police officers, social workers and health professionals from various parts of the country, and also one representative from the CPS. I also tracked down and organised interviews with a number of people who claimed to have been falsely accused of abuse, through an organisation set up to offer support to such people.

Hopefully by interviewing people from both sides I would be able to obtain an unbiased study, and this was where I needed to put my own feelings and attitudes to one side. I had formed my own opinion of the professionals involved in my case, and I think I probably went into the study assuming that all professionals in similar positions would leave me with the same rather negative feelings.

But I was actually pleasantly surprised, and most of the people I talked to did appreciate the research I was doing and seemed to accept that during the course of their work they may come across false allegations, for all sorts of different reasons. They had no real option but to put the needs of the child first, and by so doing there would always be a risk that others might be unnecessarily involved along the way, whether because of a child making a false allegation or perhaps the professionals themselves getting it wrong and accusing the wrong person. I was fascinated to listen to what these people had to say, although most were in fairly senior positions and admitted they were no longer directly involved with child abuse cases.

What was even more interesting to me was listening to the stories of those claiming to have been unnecessarily caught up in the abuse investigations, or falsely accused.

I understood and sympathised with a great deal of what was said by many of these people; they had also been hurt greatly and were very damaged individuals. I will admit, though, that one or two of the stories did concern me and I couldn't help but wonder whether these individuals really had done nothing wrong. But that was not for me to judge. I listened to and recorded what I was told; what a great dissertation I hoped to be able to write.

Once I had completed the research, I had the arduous task of analysing the interviews and writing up my findings. I think I had to write around 60,000 words, which seemed impossible at the start. But in the end I did it and eventually, after around three years of hard work, I passed my degree with flying colours. It felt like another huge achievement, especially knowing that my study would sit in the university library for years to come.

Seven

Before I finished my Master's degree, I had already started to think about what I would do next. As far as I was aware, my university friends were still teaching, but over time we had all lost touch with each other. I guess that was probably inevitable in the end, and perhaps we didn't really have a great deal in common other than the fact that we had all wanted to be teachers.

I had thought about studying for the highest degree possible, a doctorate, but in all honesty the only reason for doing this would have been to avoid the inevitable – work. I think my parents had worked this out, though, and while I know they would have continued to support me financially, they tried to encourage me to look for a job. I was now, after all, twenty-six years old! But for me, looking for work wasn't an easy task to be faced with. I still had absolutely no self-confidence or self-worth. Why on earth would anybody want to employ me, was my thinking. I knew that I was clever, that I was able to do most things I set my mind to, but unfortunately none of these qualities mattered when the mere thought of leaving the house created severe panic and anxiety.

This hang-up may not seem to make sense to an outsider, as I had just spent three years studying very diligently, going out and about interviewing strangers and driving all over the country doing so. I must have had a degree of confidence to have coped with all of this. But the fact was that I was now living back at home, just a few hundred yards from where Sally and her family lived, and for me this was an extremely traumatic environment to be in, and would again have a detrimental effect on my wellbeing.

My parents and I had talked numerous times about selling the house and moving away somewhere to make a fresh start, but I had refused categorically. It was our home, and for many years we had been very happy there. My parents and I both had friends there. Besides which, I believed strongly that if we left it would look as if we were running away, or even as if I was guilty. No, we were going to stay put, stand our ground, no matter how hard it got.

And over the years, from time to time, it was very hard, probably as hard for my parents watching me suffer as it was for me. Despite achieving two degrees, I still felt totally worthless, and felt at times as if the world might be a better place without me. I experienced deep depressions and suicidal thoughts on quite a few occasions. It was during these times that I had relied heavily on Laura in particular, and she always came to my rescue. But she knew there was nothing she could do to help practically; she could only listen, while I would repeat the same sorrowful story.

Much of my sadness centred around the way I felt my life had been affected, particularly as far as my career was concerned. While there was nothing practical stopping me from taking up a teaching post, there was something emotional stopping me: my hang-up with children and the absolute fear that the same thing could happen all over again. It was just not an option. I would never ever put myself in that position again. Not only that, but, I felt too that my personal life would never be normal. I had such a desire for children but had been left feeling unsure I would be allowed to keep my children if I did ever have any. Having a boyfriend seemed pointless; I could never expect anyone to cope with my situation.

I actually ended up falling quite by accident in to my first – and only – job. My dad and a friend of his had set up their own company a few months after dad had taken early retirement. Tragically, his business partner friend died very suddenly and unexpectedly, leaving dad to try to keep things going, as by this time they were employing several others too. This happened within weeks of my graduation, and as I was free I offered to help dad out in the short term, until he was able to manage things on his own. But that didn't ever happen. Slowly, over a period of several months, I started to take on a greater role within the company, until in the end I was offered a full-time position. I'm a great believer in fate, and while I would never have wished for anything bad to happen to his business partner, I seemed to have been in the right place at the right time so to speak; and for me this job opportunity was perfect. It meant that I did not have to somehow try to summon the courage to go to any interviews, and this was a huge weight off my shoulders. I had already been invited for one interview following a recent job application, but I had only managed to drive halfway there before turning round and going back home. Panic and paranoia had both reared their ugly heads once more.

So my life was now reasonably settled. I had a job, albeit an ill-paid one! Dad had insisted on starting me off at the bottom, just as he would have done with any new employee. I did eventually manage to save enough money to put a deposit on a house, though, and for the second time in my life I moved away from home. The house I bought was about twenty miles away from where my parents lived. I needed to be relatively close, as our office was at their house, but I also felt I would be happier living some distance from the memories of Sally and Jim.

But even now I felt so different from any other person of my age. I didn't function normally, and I certainly didn't socialise as most people my age did. I was much happier spending the evenings and weekends at home reading a book or watching television. I had friends, but I had struggled with paranoia so much that I found it impossible to trust anybody any more. I did not believe that anyone would want me in their lives, not even people I had known for many years. Laura and Martha remained firm friends though; they accepted me for the damaged person I was, and knew that there would be times I would reach out to them for friendship and support, and times when I would retreat and need time on my own. They would not allow me to push them away, though, and spent many occasions offering reassurances that they did want me in their lives. I suppose this was the aftermath of everything that had happened.

My one love was my dog. I had wanted a dog for as long as I can remember, so when I moved into my own house I had bought a beautiful black labrador puppy and called her Nell. She was amazing, more human than some humans; she and I spent many years happily walking for miles and miles, not seeing a soul, content being just the two of us. She was a great friend and comfort.

Through the research I did for my Master's degree I met

a number of like-minded people, all keen to do something to help others going through false abuse allegations. Once I had completed my dissertation and been awarded the degree, I decided to approach one or two of these people again, as I too felt that my experiences might benefit other people, if only to prevent them feeling as alone as I had felt throughout. These people came from all walks of life. Some had been at the centre of a false allegation. Others were relatives of people who had been accused. But we all had this one thing in common – there was nobody else in the world who could understand what we had been through.

We made it our mission to establish an organisation whose primary aim would be to offer support for others going through a false allegation, and quite quickly we had successfully set up our new group. Between us we knew a lot of useful people, and we managed to get a website and national telephone helpline set up almost overnight. We had no idea what would happen from here, but gradually and with the support of other organisations, our name became known and people started turning to us for support.

Three or four of us took it in turns to man the helpline during the evenings only as we all worked in the daytime, and thanks to modern technology we were able to do this from the comfort of our own homes. There were some evenings when we didn't receive any calls, others when we were inundated. We received calls from all sorts of people, all of them facing an allegation or knowing somebody who was. The vast majority of people calling us were male, I didn't ever come across any women facing allegations; I am unsure whether any of us did.

One call has stuck in my mind for all these years. It

was from a heavily pregnant lady. She told me that she had received a letter from the social services telling her that her baby would be taken in to care as soon as it was born. During the course of our chat I discovered that an allegation had been made against her partner, relating to a child from a previous relationship. The allegation was unfounded, the caller said, her partner had only ever had an informal chat with the police, there had been no arrest or charges brought, yet this huge decision had been made about the unborn child. This decision would have been made by the social services, and a great many of our calls concerned the involvement of the social services, much more so than the police in fact. I can still remember the sadness and fear expressed by this lady. She was so scared about what was going to happen, at what should have been a happy and exciting time preparing for her baby's arrival.

The nature of this call was not unusual, though; we had many similar calls, all just differing slightly. All we could do was listen and offer reassurance that they were not alone. I talked about my own experiences if I thought too that this might help, and I have no doubt that it did. This was the first time for almost all callers that they had opened up to anybody.

Over time the organisation grew and, in addition to offering emotional support, we were also able to start offering the names of solicitors who were known to have handled similar cases, and who had become 'specialists' in the area of false allegations. We started to produce information booklets, and also attended conferences in an attempt to highlight false allegations as a real problem within society.

I was even approached by television programmes and magazines, requesting interviews, and I appeared on four shows. I was interviewed by an international news channel, and one magazine wrote a lengthy article about my experiences. What happened to me created a fair amount of interest, and I think my willingness to talk openly about it helped the organisation in its quest to reach out to people in this situation everywhere.

At around this time I enrolled in a night course at our local college. Over a period of several weeks I completed a basic course in counselling. I felt I needed to learn some of the fundamental skills required to converse with vulnerable people, and the course turned out to be invaluable for the work I was doing with the organisation.

I will never forget one young man in particular, who first made contact with us through the helpline late one evening. I think he must have talked to not only me but also several of my colleagues, over a period of several months; he was in a desperate situation and needed a great deal of emotional support. Our role on the helpline was to listen and between us we spent hours and hours listening to this young caller.

He was a GP in one of the UK's large cities, and by the time he found us he had already been charged with raping a young lady he knew quite well. His family lived abroad and he had nobody to support him at all. One of my colleagues and I met him several times before his trial and I then offered to support his family, who were planning to travel to the UK from their home country, throughout the trial. I was able to keep them up to speed with what was happening, and I'm sure they were grateful for my help. This was the first trial I had ever attended, and it was quite a traumatic experience for me as well as for them. By this time I had become very fond of our caller, we had spent much time together, so I was now watching a friend go through so much, and so publicly too. Sadly, after the two-week trial, he was convicted of rape and sent to prison for just under five years. I remember his sister, who had been sitting beside me, collapse on to the floor in a crumpled heap, her agonising screams piercing the court room. None of us could quite believe the jury's decision.

To this day I do not believe that he raped the girl. It would obviously be inappropriate for me to discuss specific details of the case, but the evidence just did not stack up.

Following his conviction, the sister remained in the UK for several months, determined to try to help her brother. I offered her a place to live, I had a spare bedroom, and so she lived with me and Nell for a few months, spending her time talking to solicitors and barristers, trying to find any way of helping her brother. But it turned out to be a fruitless exercise. Getting a conviction overturned, or at least achieving an appeal, is an extremely difficult process requiring new previously unheard evidence, a process that demands a great deal of time and money. So he remained in prison. I visited him several times, and each time his mental health had deteriorated. After just a few months he was a shell of a man. I bought him books to read to try to keep his mind active, but I really believe that he had given up the day he was convicted. Sadly he eventually refused to see me, and our contact stopped. I was devastated but had to respect his decision. I just hoped that he would continue to allow his sister to visit. She had decided to remain in the UK for as long as she could. When she eventually found somewhere more permanent to live, nearer to the prison, she moved out and over time we too lost touch with each other.

Several years later, out of the blue, my telephone rang. It was this same young man. He had been released from prison, and had been immediately deported back to his home country. He had tracked me down and was phoning to say thank you for my help all those years ago. I cried and cried, so relieved to hear his voice and to know that he had somehow survived his ordeal. I knew that his life would never be the same, and that we would probably never meet again. But I was thankful to him for finding me and letting me know that he was OK as I had worried so much that he would not survive harsh prison life, especially as a convicted rapist. I will never forget him. Perhaps one day I will try to find him. It would be nice to know that he has managed to find some joy in his life.

Through our organisation I had at last found a way of dealing with my own life and personal hang-ups. I felt that I was in some small way able to help others, which I know from the feedback we received was much appreciated. I no longer felt as alone as I had; there were many others feeling the same way I did and in actual fact I came into contact with many people over the years who had had to deal with far worse situations than I had.

I am so proud of the group I helped to establish and although I am not involved in its running today, it still fills me with great happiness to know that it continues to help people in need.

Partly as a result of my time with the organisation, meeting and talking to so many people all with different experiences to share, and partly because of my own curiosity, I decided to apply to the social services for copies of all their paperwork relating to the abuse investigation involving Sarah. I had heard some horror stories while working at the organisation from people who had done the same thing following their own cases. They had found all kinds of factually incorrect information being held on files about them, which concerned me about my own files. I knew that I would only receive information about myself; nothing about Sarah or any other party would be released.

At around the same time, I decided to approach my GP with a view to accessing my health records too, as I thought it likely that something may also have been written on these that referred back to the abuse investigation. I somehow felt the need to know how I was being portrayed, and had an absolute determination for whatever records there were to be accurate. I hated the thought that my character might be blemished. GP's notes had not been computerised at this time, and so it was relatively easy for my GP to provide me with the notes to read.

What I found was devastating. There was just one comment that was significant to all that had happened, but boy was it a tough one to digest. All of the main notes were dull, grey or cream in colour, all bar one sheet, which was a fairly vivid green. I am unsure what other information this sheet contained; all I do remember is that it seemed to stick out above the rest of the notes, as if it was a little bit longer. At the top of this green piece of paper it stated, "ACCUSED OF SEXUAL ABUSE. CANCELLED." I felt physically sick. It was there for everyone to see.

I went home and tried to take on board what I had seen on my notes, but having seen what was written, there was just no way I could ignore it. I knew too that I could never face going to the surgery ever again. I could not accept that "cancelled" would mean the previous part of the statement being ignored. Of course it wouldn't. I would forever be a suspected child abuser, and I could not accept that or move on with my life knowing that people would look at me with this at the forefront of their minds. I had to summon the courage to ask my GP to remove the statement. And thank goodness there are some reasonable people in this world. The statement, in its entirety, was removed from my notes.

There was quite some delay initially with my social services request, but this was because I was unaware of the correct protocols, (or indeed that the process was called a Subject Access Request) which needed to be followed precisely in order for my request to be dealt with. Interestingly, though, even after I got to grips with this, there still appeared to be some reluctance to provide me with any documents. At first I was told that nothing had been found, but after persisting I did eventually receive various documents, albeit in dribs and drabs and over a period of some months. I had to enlist the help of the Data Protection Commissioner, a body set up to assist with these kinds of issues, and it was only due to their contact with the social services that most of the information I'd been asking for was eventually sent to me. I was interested to find out that there was no actual file held in my name; all information was contained within Sarah's file.

Having been provided with everything they told me I was entitled to, I knew there remained a number of significant documents, but the social services claimed they no longer existed. This infuriated and worried me – I knew for a fact that certain meetings had taken place, yet any minutes had miraculously disappeared.

Much of the documentation that I did eventually receive contained blacked-out sections, and it was explained that these sections contained information that I was not entitled to see. However, some of these sections were still reasonably easy to read! I probably should not even have tried but I was intrigued to know what I was not being allowed to see, as I'm sure anybody else in the same boat would have been. I wasn't able to read everything, but I could pick out small snippets. Interestingly, Sally and Jim had made some particularly unkind comments about my family; I suppose this had been part of their quest to incriminate me, by painting a pretty poor image of my family relationships and the way we lived our lives. What I read only served to clarify the way in which their attitude towards me had changed, almost overnight. It was hurtful to say the least, and so I decided that, rather than rake up the past, I would read only the material that I was supposed to be reading. And as it turned out, this was hard enough.

Much of what I received I already had copies of, but there were some documents that I was seeing for the first time. Of particular interest were several documents that had been written by a female social worker whose name I had not come across before – as far as I had been aware, the only social worker involved had been Mr Smith. I thought that perhaps Sarah must have been assigned a social worker of her own as a result of this investigation, and these documents must have been written by that lady.

She seemed to have jotted down notes each time she saw Sarah or her parents. One note talks about Sarah's teacher having to stay at the hospital with Sarah until very late at night, stating that Sally had had to leave the hospital in order to get me to leave too. I do remember the teacher visiting, but I had no idea at the time that the purpose of her visit had been to help Sally get me away from Sarah. My recollection is very different; I'm sure the teacher called at the hospital for a flitting visit only, and I'm sure Sally wasn't there at the time of her visit. Another written note from the time that Sarah was in hospital states that the social worker had advised Sally not to leave me on my own with Sarah. And a further note stated clearly that Sally and Jim had told her I was still going to the house following Sarah's hospitalisation, and that they wanted everything to remain normal until after Sarah had been interviewed. This confirmed my thoughts at the time, that Sally had indeed been trying to keep things the same.

The social worker, however, continued by stating her belief that I should not be left alone with any of the children. Why on earth would she say this so early on in the investigation? The only evidence suggesting that Sarah had been abused, prior to the police interviews, was medical evidence, and that did not implicate anybody. Why then would she say that I should not be left alone with them, unless the idea that I had committed the alleged offence had already been decided? I cannot help but wonder whether this social worker planted the idea in Sally and Jim's mind that I might be the alleged abuser, or whether perhaps Sally and Jim planted the idea in hers. Whichever way round, it is obvious from the notes kept by this lady that this happened within just a day or two of the abuse concerns having been raised.

There were further notes, made by the same social worker, indicating that after her police interview Sarah continued to "tell" her parents that I had abused her. It was also alleged that Sarah wanted my photograph removed from her talking machine, and she had also apparently developed a fear of the family's downstairs toilet. If these points were highlighted during the meeting that had made the decision to notify my university, I suppose I could understand now to a greater degree why that decision had been made. But I now saw Sally and Jim in a completely different light, and I was sure that things had been made up or at least blown out of all proportion during the investigation in order that the finger could be pointed at me.

The significance of the downstairs toilet is that Sarah used this one rather than the upstairs one each time she needed to go to the loo. On the many occasions when she was constipated, Sally knew if one of us could get her to laugh while sitting on the loo, it might do the trick. If I was at the house, the job of getting Sarah to laugh was inevitably given to me and I would therefore accompany her to the loo. The suggestion that Sarah had subsequently developed a fear of the downstairs loo seems to have been put forward as further indication that I had abused Sarah, and in that specific room. But the room was tiny. When I did take Sarah to the loo, I would sit on the floor outside the room with the door open; there just would not have been enough room for me to go in with her and close the door. Sadly these additional details, which I feel were significant, appear either not to have been mentioned, or else ignored.

This same social worker also noted her concerns about the respite home where I had carried out some voluntary work. I went on to do some occasional bank work there, which was paid, but I hated it. I was always asked to work nights, and I found it virtually impossible to stay awake. The reason I had done some voluntary work at the home had been to gain experience with the children, but working nights was nothing other than hard work. I hardly ever saw any children; they would be fast asleep. So the social worker need not have worried that I might still be working there, but it worried me reading her comments that even though the decision to inform organisations about the allegation against me had been overturned, perhaps she might have gone against this decision had she felt it necessary.

It was also clear from the information I was given that Sally and Jim had chosen not to provide any details either about the first time Sarah and I saw each other following her stay in hospital. This had been a brief encounter, admittedly, but Sarah had been pleased to see me and had reached out her hand for me to hold. However, Sally and Jim had told the social worker that the first time I saw Sarah was the time she had reacted badly towards me. Why would they do this? There were further comments by this same female social worker, stating, "I have dealt with a number of sexual abuse investigations and I felt fairly certain in this case that Sarah had been abused by the person she named. Her learning difficulties, if anything, made her allegations more likely to be true than those of some children, because (I am told) she can neither lie, nor can she hold two ideas in her head at one time..."

For me these notes are particularly significant, as this woman, who I had never met, is clearly stating her belief that I had abused Sarah. Surely that kind of decision could not be made without meeting me? Upon what could she have based her belief, except from information provided by Sally and Jim? Her earlier notes, from the time that Sarah was still in hospital and the possibility of abuse had only just been raised, also appear to imply that I was presumed to be the guilty party. I cannot understand at all how she had reached this conclusion, not least because she had not met me, but also because there was absolutely nothing other than opportunity upon which she could have made her judgements. At this stage I had not been interviewed, and neither had Sarah. It is hugely concerning that her notes might have been used as evidence in this case.

In addition to this, she states clearly that Sarah was

unable to process two ideas, yet the police had readily accepted Sarah using two ideas during her police interview; she had pressed my photograph and then put her hands between her legs. Surely the social worker's statement conflicted completely with Sarah's responses during the police interview. Why then did they not consider the idea that she might be primed? Having been interviewed once already, Sally and Jim would have known what questions Sarah was going to be asked the second time; her responses could easily have been rehearsed before the second interview was ever carried out.

I wasn't upset any more. Years had passed, and I had seen Sally and Jim's true colours. No, I was by now extremely angry, not just that I had been dragged through the mill by the police and social services all those years ago, but more so because my life had been devastated by what had happened. I was quite a bitter and resentful person, too. Why did this have to happen to me, was my predominant thought these days.

I knew there was no turning back the clock. I just needed to make the most of what I had now. But having seen what was written about me, I could not bring myself to walk away. I wanted this information to be destroyed, or at the very least for all the inaccuracies to be amended.

I started to do some research, and found a firm of solicitors that I thought might be able to help me. I made contact and they agreed to assist. It would be costly, I knew, but by now I was earning a good living, and was more than prepared to spend some of my savings on something so important. So, over the next few months, various letters were sent between my solicitor and the solicitor representing the social services. My solicitor and I also met with a barrister who had a specific interest in data protection. Her advice was invaluable, although I think she felt we were faced with an uphill battle.

We were invited to a meeting with the Head of Social Care (who, interestingly, had been the District Children and Families Manager at the time of the investigation), accompanied by the social services' own solicitor. To give them credit, this meeting was beneficial in that we were given the time we needed to explain our concerns, and we left believing that the issues we had raised had been taken on board. But whether or not any changes would be made we would not know for some weeks to come. I wanted all references to my name to be erased; but I knew that this was highly unlikely to be agreed. However, if the social services agreed to amend what was written or to include additional documents stating my belief that certain comments were inaccurate, and in some cases completely incorrect, that was a compromise I would be prepared to accept. I also wanted all missing documentation to be provided.

Unfortunately, we were never able to get the agreement of the social services to destroy any information held about me, partly because that would have gone against their policies, but also because it would also have meant destroying information they held about Sarah. My name formed part of her file, and this would not be destroyed until she had reached a certain age. Social services also continued to claim that certain documents no longer existed, which I still found hard to believe.

However, after a number of months of toing and froing, the social services did eventually agree to the inclusion of a statement in Sarah's file that read, "A full investigation of allegations of child abuse against Jessie Kyd were investigated and were concluded to be without foundation." Anyone reading the file would be directed to this statement at each and every relevant point. I suppose this was probably as much as we might have hoped for, although my solicitor did feel we might achieve even more than this if I was prepared to continue to push the matter for a while longer.

For me, though, this was the end of the road. I was exhausted and had reached the point when I knew it was time to walk away from this horrible situation. It had haunted me the last few years, at the expense of everything. Friends had spent time going out, some had met their future husbands, got married and some had even had children of their own. What had I done? I had become almost obsessed with righting the wrongs of what had happened to me. There was nothing I could do to help Sarah; I had tried, but nobody would listen. I had no choice but to walk away from her.

So instead I determined to make the situation better for myself, and to somehow try to find a way of living a normal existence. I could not escape from the horrors of what had happened – nobody could erase these from my memory, they would remain there for ever. But with the help of various people I had managed to right some of the wrongs and I did eventually receive a letter from the social services that stated:

"I confirm, on behalf of ******* (the name of the social services department has been blanked out here for the purpose of the book), that you are not considered a risk to children following the investigations…"

This was, again, probably as much as I could hope for. It wasn't perfect, but at least it provided me with some reassurances and would hopefully enable me to move forward with my life.

Eight

Present Day

Life was good, but it could still have been better.

I didn't ever meet my Mr Right – or if I did some place along the way, I didn't realise it! I'd had the occasional boyfriend and was in fact engaged briefly, but my insecurities and paranoia didn't ever allow me to trust any of them or really allow them to get to know me properly. Deep down I think the past continued to haunt me, and the natural transition from relationship to marriage to having children just wasn't ever going to be an option for me, so I could see no real point in bothering with relationships. The sadness I felt knowing that, if I did have children, they might be taken away from me, was at times unbearable, so in some ways it was easier to live a life that didn't involve the complications of relationships and what might have been.

I have always been an open and honest person, and even when I was in one fairly serious relationship I still found it virtually impossible to allow him to get close to me; I was holding something that had been such a huge part of my life back from him and it just didn't feel right.

I explored the possibility of becoming a foster carer. My

love of children would never disappear, and I thought that perhaps this avenue might provide a little of what I would otherwise never have, as well as giving me an additional income. However, my openness and honesty once again worked against me. I was part way through the introductory 'getting to know you' phase with the fostering agency and I told them what had happened to me, thinking that it might actually make me a more suitable candidate. Sadly, though, I was wrong, and the fostering agency didn't even bother to contact me in person to let me know that I was deemed unsuitable to progress any further; instead they just sent me a rather impersonal letter. The inference was that they were doing me a favour by their actions, but I'm really not sure about that. I think it is much more likely that they didn't want to take any risks. But again, looking back now that I have a much more positive outlook on life, I think they probably did do me a favour; taking potentially damaged children into my home might just have created more problems than I needed.

One day, some months later, I bumped into an old friend I hadn't seen for quite a while. We'd known each other for many years; he had once lived in a nearby village and our mutual love of fast cars had brought us together on many occasions. We'd met up for cups of tea together and had had chats about cars as well as all sorts of other things. He was an interesting man and I liked him and his wife very much. I had eventually confided in him and he knew how overwhelmingly sad I felt at not being able to fulfil my lifelong dream of having children. On this particular day we had talked for hours while drinking much tea, and I came away with a spring in my step; my mind was full of exciting thoughts about my future. I had an idea and needed to talk to my parents about it.

I remember the conversation as if it was yesterday. My parents sat in silence listening to me explaining what I was proposing to do. They were concerned, naturally, as all parents would be – and perhaps my parents were now more protective towards me as a result of what had happened. Yet they offered their complete support, just as they always had.

I am very lucky to have such amazing parents. The previous years had taken their toll on mum and dad, and in particular on my mum's health. Generally speaking, after the investigation people had continued to be friendly towards them but those same people didn't always want to talk to me, which made it very awkward. Needless to say, my parents' loyalty towards me was always second to none, although some of their 'friends' did fall by the wayside. They just weren't interested in people who were prepared to listen to the gossip. This had been hard on us all, but I think as you get older stressful situations can have a longer-lasting effect. I hated the fact that the abuse investigation really had caused untold stresses and strains for them both.

A few months later, at the age of thirty, having made sure that I had the full support of my parents, I moved to France. I had decided, with the help of my old friend and plenty of cups of tea, that I wanted to buy a house and make a new life for myself over there. I loved the country, having spent many happy summers there with my parents when I was growing up. We hadn't ever bothered holidaying in other countries; there were so many beautiful regions in France, each one so different to the last one we had visited. I had loved learning French at school too, and had always achieved better results in languages than any other subjects.

So I spent the summer following my thirtieth birthday

in glorious France, exploring various areas and viewing properties with local estate agents. Such fun – apart from anything, it was fascinating looking around such different properties. Some were fairly run-down, but still advertised by the French agents as habitable! This always made me laugh. Their idea of what was habitable and mine couldn't have been more different. Some properties I loved but they were in the wrong location; others were not so great but located in a stunning setting. That was Sod's Law!

I thoroughly enjoyed every minute of my time there that summer. I had gone on my own, and had taken the ferry across to France and then driven to the areas I wanted to explore. I felt so relaxed and carefree. There was no anxiety and no paranoia. For the first time in a very long time I felt content. I knew I was making the right decision.

One house that I viewed fairly early on in my search stuck in my mind, and I asked to see it a second time before I left to return to the UK. It was quirky to say the least, an old detached cottage with huge rooms and a magnificent fireplace. I could picture myself here in the wintertime, curled up in front of the wood burner that I would need to install. There was a large barn too, and a field. This seemed to be the norm with most properties I viewed; I didn't need a barn or field, but they were often part of the deal. I decided that this was the house for me; by my standards it was exceptionally cheap, and I knew I could afford it.

By this time I had become a director of dad's company, and was a shareholder too. Dad was taking more of a back seat these days, but there were two other directors. We also employed more than forty consultants. Money just wasn't an issue for me, which was great. I was intending to carry on working from a home office in France. Most of my work was telephone and internet based anyway, so location really didn't matter. I would need to return to the UK for the occasional business meeting, but that was fine; I could combine these visits with catching up with family and friends.

My offer on the house was accepted; it had been on the market for some time and I knew the vendor wanted to move sooner rather than later. Before too long I found myself preparing for the big move, all alone except for my dog Nell, but terribly excited about the new life I might lead. I hired a huge lorry to take all of my belongings over on the ferry. Hopefully I could leave the past behind me and start a new life. At least that was my plan, and I intended to stick to it.

And stick to it I did. I spent several very happy years in the house I bought. I had various bits of work done, and I became a fluent French speaker. I did of course make mistakes from time to time, but none as bad as my poor dad. My parents would visit regularly, and dad always made every effort to use the lingo. He was amazingly efficient, though, at getting mixed up, and would frequently have us in tears from laughing so much at his mistakes. I decorated and had plans drawn up to renovate the barn to make two holiday cottages.

I also met some fabulous people, both French and English. They got to know me and I got to know them. I didn't ever talk about what had happened to me, but that was for the best. I didn't expect anybody to understand, and somehow it had become an insignificant part of my past. I found again a little bit of the confidence I'd once had, and that helped me form lovely friendships with many people. Life was simple, but it was happy. I had a good social life, for the first time in a long time, and I loved every minute of my time in this beautiful country.

After four amazing years, I decided to sell the house. I felt that it was time for a change once more. I had started to miss my family and friends, my parents and Laura especially. They had all visited many times, but the house always felt very empty when they left to go home, and I was worried that my old depression might rear its ugly head again. Winters in France were lonely times; the French seem to hibernate for several months on end, and so I would rely on the handful of English friends I had for company. It wasn't ideal; I realised that I needed to be around people and to be busy.

Today I find myself living back in the UK, ironically not all that far from where I lived with my parents at the time of the abuse investigation. But time has moved on, and it is true what people say – time is a great healer. I do still struggle with paranoia, but I have learned to deal with it more effectively, and thankfully it no longer bothers me as it once did. From time to time there are still very dark moments when I struggle, but I am overwhelmed by the continued support of some very special people. Sally and Jim, although they no longer run the wool shop, still live nearby too. I see them from time to time and we pass by each other but they never make eye contact. I feel no anger towards them now; all I feel is pity and some sadness. They too had a lot to deal with, and while they did not deal with the situation well as far as I was concerned, they still had to go through a very traumatic time, and I'm sure they must feel some degree of pain even today. These things don't ever go away completely.

There is no forgiveness, though. For whatever reason, they sat and knowingly watched me trying to deal with everything that was thrown my way, and I don't think there will ever be a time when I can forgive them. Forget maybe, but not forgive.

The very best news of all is that I am now the mother of three beautiful children.

I still haven't met Mr Right, but in this day and age that really doesn't matter. I have been blessed, and my children have transformed my world.

The moment my first-born son arrived in the world and I held him in my arms, I knew that everything was going to be OK. He isn't old enough to know it yet, but he saved my life. I would never have been able to carry on without fulfilling my dream of becoming a mother.

I will forever be grateful to their father for his belief in me and for giving me the greatest gift ever. They will grow up knowing that they must treat others the way they would like to be treated, and as long as they go out into this big scary world with kindness, and a level head on their shoulders, they will be just fine. I will admit, though, to being somewhat overprotective; I think this was inevitable considering everything that has happened in my life and one day in the future they will hopefully understand!

And the best news of all is that the social services haven't bothered me once. My eldest son was born in France, and actually this was part of my reason for moving over there when I did. I wasn't prepared to allow that one social worker and his spiteful comments to take over my life and govern my future. I knew when I moved there that I was going to have a child, and that I would remain in France forever if that was what it took to be left alone and for me and my new family to be able to live our lives peacefully. I was never going to allow my child to be taken away from me. The helpline call I took from the very frightened pregnant lady I talked about earlier had stayed with me all these years. Her fear was unimaginable and I knew without any shadow of a doubt that I would not cope with the same situation, faced with having my child taken from me. I would do whatever I could to protect myself and my son.

But I did miss my parents and my closest friends back in the UK terribly, hence the eventual decision to move back. But before doing so, I needed to ensure that it would be safe. Safe in as much as knowing that my child would not be taken away from me as soon as I set foot on English soil. I wasn't entirely sure how to go about this, but as a first port of call I visited my GP in the UK to seek his advice, explaining my desire to move back home. I told him of my fears that my son would be taken away from me. This would not happen, he told me. I would be treated exactly the same way as any other parent; the only time this would change was if any concerns about my child's welfare were raised. While this was extremely reassuring to hear, could I really believe what he was telling me? Professional people, people supposedly trained to deal with cases such Sarah's, had all once stood together and dismissed me. They had all seemed to believe that I had harmed Sarah, so much so that they were prepared to watch my career come to an end before it had even begun. Why, ten years on, should I believe that anything had changed?

However, if I wanted to come home, I had no choice but to believe what I had been told. It was a risk I had to be prepared to take. I knew I was a good mother and I knew that I would fight should anybody try to say otherwise. There wasn't really any decision to make – I knew in my heart of hearts that I wanted to be close to my family and friends again. I was petrified, though, on the journey back to the UK. It was a long journey, and I had plenty of time to imagine all sorts. I don't really know what I was expecting, but I do remember picturing a gang of social workers stopping the car the minute we got off the ferry and whisking my child away! My imagination was working overtime, I know, but I did have nightmares about it for weeks beforehand.

I am very happy to be able to say that, since arriving back in the UK around eight years ago, I have been left alone to get on with my life. My children are my life now; everything else a dim and distant memory that I have at last been able to put to bed, for most of the time. There are still bad days from time to time, and there probably always will be. I try to remain positive and to be grateful for the good things in my life, but there is no denying that my life has not turned out as I had always hoped it would. There have been many times over the years when I have needed more support than my friends and family were able to give, and they would be shocked to know just how low I have felt at times. For me though, even plucking up the courage to ask for help from a professional felt like too much of a risk even in recent years; convinced that my emotional weakness would reflect badly on me as a parent I have never sought help from anybody. I don't think anyone could experience the trauma I experienced without some permanent scarring at the end of it but the absolute fear that somebody somewhere might interpret my scars as something other than damage caused by this dreadful experience, has prevented me from asking for help.

These days I spend as much quality time with my children as I can and work fits in around them. Children are amazingly therapeutic and a great distraction on a bad day.

It's all about priorities and for me earning money is much less important than it once was.

I stayed with my dad's business for several more enjoyable years, and gradually worked my way up to the top. Although the work was not a field that had ever appealed to me, through my work I have been able to build up my confidence, having to attend important meetings, interviewing potential staff and generally keeping the business running smoothly following my dad's retirement.

But children aren't children for long, and I too retired from the company some years ago. I work now only on a casual consultancy basis. I am determined to enjoy every possible minute with my children, and hopefully they will appreciate this as they get older. They may not have every modern gadget that some of their friends have, but I have sacrificed earning a good living to be with them, and one day, although perhaps not until they themselves are parents, I hope they will see that I did the right thing.

I have an amazing circle of friends, too. I am at last comfortable in the company of other peoples' children; this was a huge hurdle that I needed to overcome. Thanks to my children having many friends between them, I have been thrown in at the deep end but I no longer have the concern I once had that one of these children, or their parents, might accuse me of abuse. And that is an amazing feeling to have.

Laura, her husband and daughter remain a huge part of my life, even though they live quite a way from us. She is the best friend in the world, and I will be grateful to her for her support forever. Ironically, she recently trained in social work, and I just know that she will be a brilliant social worker (as social workers go!). Thankfully our friendship can weather anything; we sat and talked at length about her desire to train in social work some time before she eventually put in her application; she was worried, I know, that this might impact on our friendship, as my opinion of social workers was so tainted by that one man all those years ago. Laura knows better than anyone that his comments completely altered the course of my life.

But the truth of the matter now is that my life is far better than ever it would have been had this sad situation not occurred. I do wonder if I would ever have passed my degree course, let alone gone on to achieve a second one, had I just plodded on working for Sarah's family.

I am sad that the truth of what did or did not happen to Sarah has never been properly resolved. Or perhaps it has been and I just don't know about it. I am certain if anybody else was ever arrested by the police that I might have heard about it, but who knows. I can but hope, especially that all of the people who were so ready to label me a child abuser may after all this time have had second thoughts and realised that I was in fact a perfect scapegoat (by referring to myself as a scapegoat I must make it clear that I am in no way implying anybody else's guilt, just that I was wrongly blamed for somebody's wrongdoing, if indeed Sarah had been abused).

Sarah is still alive today, more than twenty years later. I don't know what had happened to make Sally and Jim report to the police that she did not have much longer to live; perhaps this was information they had been given by the specialists who kept an eye on her. I guess all that matters is that she is still around and I hope so much that she is happy.

I have such fond memories of the wonderful times we had, and will remember them for ever. Our last moments together were brief but cherished – by us both, I'm sure. I still pray that she hadn't been abused and everything that happened was just one huge mistake. But what a mistake to make. Whatever happened to 'innocent until proven guilty'?

The letter I eventually received from the social services is as close as I will ever get to an apology, and it is also probably as close as I will ever get to an acknowledgement that I did not do anything wrong. The truth is, though, not even an apology can give me back the life I should have had.

It would be amazing to see my book added to the reading list of every trainee social worker, and every other professional involved in child protection, in the hope that lessons can be learned for the future and the same mistakes not repeated. I would be thrilled.

If you are innocent, you must hold your head high as you walk down the street. It doesn't matter what anybody else thinks, however much their comments might hurt at the time. You know the truth; take a deep breath, think positive thoughts and look at people with a smile on your face. You are as good as them, and at the end of the day you are in fact a better person than they are – because your experiences have taught you never to judge people the way you were judged.

Epilogue

Since completing my book there has been a frustrating development after all these years which I feel I must talk about.

Writing this story has been my intention for many years, and I have somehow managed to put pen to paper much sooner than I ever imagined I would. My children take up all of my time these days and I didn't think I would be able to do this until further down the line. But I have, and I feel more than ready for people to read about what happened to me.

My main concern all along has been my children, and how they would cope with knowing about my past; they will inevitably find out about it once my book is publicly available. It has always been my plan to talk to them about this period of my life one day, but I had never really considered what age would be appropriate.

Some months ago I telephoned my health visitor, the purpose of my call being to ask if she might point me in the direction of a professional person or organisation that might be able to advise if my oldest son in particular is likely to be able to deal with the content of my book. I had no hesitation about contacting her, as she has in the past always been able to provide very useful information about various issues.

Unfortunately, though, the outcome of this particular telephone conversation was not as I had hoped it might be. My health visitor asked what the book is about, and without thinking about any possible consequences, I told her. She asked further questions, and I answered, again without thinking.

At the end of our conversation, she did suggest one possible organisation that might be able to advise me about my son, but the original purpose of my call was pretty much forgotten about and instead the content of my book became the focus of my health visitor's attention.

It became apparent that she felt somewhat indignant because until this conversation she had not known anything about the allegation against me. I was living abroad when my first son was born, and she was not our health visitor when we moved back to the UK. Whether or not the health visitor assigned to us at that time knew what had happened never crossed my mind until now. Perhaps she did not know either.

Anyway, my current health visitor was somewhat put out; she said that she should have known about my past. She told me that if I had a baby girl, I might have an issue changing nappies, and her support would inevitably then be needed. I found this suggestion pretty upsetting; it had not crossed my mind for one minute that things would be any different if I had a baby girl. Perhaps my old paranoia was rearing its ugly head again, but I felt her comments hurtful and actually inappropriate.

We ended my call with the health visitor telling me that she may need to make a written record of what I had told her, not that I had written a book, but that an allegation had previously been made against me. She would need to talk to my GP, she said. I sat in silence at the end of the telephone, dumbfounded.

Unfortunately, as a result my health visitor did make notes on her records about the allegation made against me, despite every effort being made to stop this from happening. She defended this by adding that she has no concerns about my parenting. She tells me that I am a lovely mum, very attentive. But for me these additional comments are irrelevant. The allegation against me is now more than twenty years old. There have been no concerns about me since this dreadful time. I have been a parent for more than twelve of those years, and there have been no concerns about me during those twelve years either.

I could not believe that there was any justification for adding such comments; she obviously felt the need to 'cover her back', as is sadly typical of our society today. It's all about accountability and protocol. If there were any concerns at all, I would have completely understood that something would need to be written, but not until that point in time surely. There was apparently some discussion of carrying out a risk assessment on me too, as my 'disclosure' could be deemed a safeguarding issue. As I explained on the telephone to my health visitor's superior, however, I would have been reluctant to cooperate with something so ridiculous. I have always been very open and more than willing for my health visitor to call in on us, but this would have been a complete invasion of my privacy and of my children's too. There are no concerns about me or them; please leave us alone.

For months I was passed from pillar to post. Nobody seemed to want to deal with my request that the notes written by the health visitor should be removed. It became increasingly clear that nobody actually knew whose responsibility this was!

To date my children have been unaffected by my past, and I would never have returned from France had I thought for one minute that this or something similar might end up happening. I would certainly not have gone on to have more children here in the UK. I have nothing at all to hide, but I know that comments about a previous allegation against me, no matter how long ago, have the potential to affect my children greatly. We will no longer be thought of as a normal family, we will be looked at differently, and everything about us scrutinised more than it otherwise would have been. This is how false suspicions and false allegations sometimes arise.

Research I have carried out online highlights situations where health visitors have passed on their notes to schools, and this was my greatest fear, that my past will now follow my children around. It has always been my hope that they can live normal lives, unaffected by what happened to me. But this was beginning to look increasingly unlikely, and the strain I was feeling was becoming unbearable.

I do appreciate fully that there have been some awful cases in the media which have highlighted failings by health visitors and other professionals, where actual abuse has been missed, resulting in tragic deaths of children in some cases, and I do understand the thin line these people tread, but my health visitor, while needing to cover her own back, has got to know me quite well during recent years and she has met my children many times. She knows us well enough to see that nothing untoward is happening and could very easily expect that nothing untoward is ever going to happen. But she was not prepared to take that risk, even if it impacted on my life and as a consequence the life of my children. I felt my old anxieties returning, along with my paranoia. She told me she has no concerns but that somehow seemed irrelevant when the children's so far unblemished notes have been altered by adding notes about my past.

My children could see that something was upsetting me, and that in turn affects them. My oldest son is incredibly perceptive and no matter how hard I try to keep things from him, he always sees through my brave face. I believed that we as a family deserve better than this, but I was beginning to realise that perhaps the past was never going to leave us alone.

Thankfully, though, and after many, many months, I received the reassuring news that the notes made by my health visitor will now be removed. This is such a huge relief but the battle to reach this point has caused incredible upset and worry. I am exhausted too. But I refused to give in, even when I was told that I had no chance of winning. After much toing and froing I eventually found somebody who was prepared to listen to me, and the decision was finally made by the Caldicott Guardian, alongside the Information Governance team, who all work within our local health service. The paperwork I kept all these years proved invaluable too; I was able to provide the confirmation I had from social services that there was no foundation to the allegation, and this was justification enough for the removal of the notes.

My intention in writing this book has been to show that people faced with situations like mine can pull through, no matter how impossible that might seem at the time. These last few months have been tough to say the least, but I fought for something I believe in more than anything, which is justice, and I do feel that I have achieved just that. My life is amazing and I feel hugely proud of all that I have achieved and will hopefully continue to achieve.

On completion of my book, I gave it to my dad to read through; he has been encouraging me for years to put pen to paper. When he handed it back to me, with tears in his eyes, all he could bring himself to say was, "How the hell did we ever get through this?"